SUCCESSFUL DIVERSITY MANAGEMENT INITIATIVES

Patricia Arredondo

SUCCESSFUL DIVERSITY MANAGEMENT INITIATIVES

A Blueprint for Planning and Implementation

SAGE Publications
International Educational and Professional Publisher
Thousand Oaks London New Delhi

For information address:

SAGE Publications, Inc.
2455 Teller Road
Thousand Oaks, California 91320
E-mail: order@sagepub.com

SAGE Publications Ltd.
6 Bonhill Street
London EC2A 4PU
United Kingdom

SAGE Publications India Pvt. Ltd.
M-32 Market
Greater Kailash I
New Delhi 110 048 India

Printed in the United States of America

Library of Congress Cataloging-in-Publication Data

Arredondo, Patricia.
  Successful diversity management initiatives: A blueprint for planning and implementation / Patricia Arredondo.
    p. cm.
  Includes bibliographical references.
  ISBN 0-8039-7290-3 (cloth: acid-free paper).—ISBN 0-8039-7291-1 (pbk.: acid-free paper)
  1. Minorities—Employment. 2. Multiculturalism. 3. Personnel management. I. Title.
HF5549.5.M5A77   1996
658.3'041—dc20   95-50227

This book is printed on acid-free paper.

99 00 10 9 8 7 6 5 4 3

Sage Production Editor: Tricia K. Bennett
Sage Typesetter: Marion S. Warren
Sage Cover Designer: Lesa F. Valdez

Contents

Introduction

In my youth, I had the experience of working with adults in school, church, and recreational settings and learning through their example about motivating and managing people. These examples were both positive and negative. During my high school and college years, I placed myself in leadership roles, always striving to get people in extracurricular organizations to work together toward a common goal. I learned the value of teamwork and of meeting goals through well-articulated action plans. As a high school counselor and university professor, I gained a more intimate understanding of the workings . of organizational cultures—their power, impact, and influence on people. Here again, I witnessed and experienced people-to-people interactions on a number of different levels: in cliques, in response to newcomers or other individual differences, in response to authority and organizational systems, and in response to change introduced into the status quo.

In 1975, in a town in the greater Boston area well-known for its outstanding public school system, a group of newcomers arrived at the high school door. They came speaking languages other than English and with school transcripts that bore no resemblance to our report cards. In many instances, the students arrived with an adult who was

Figure I.1. Planning and Managing Diversity Initiatives
© Empowerment Workshops, Inc.

not a parent. Once the students made it past the reception desk, they needed help in designing a schedule of classes to attend. What were their abilities? How might they fit in a monolingual English-speaking classroom? What could be expected from teachers and peers? These questions were the beginning of a process to address a set of new experiences for the school organization and for personnel, from front-desk admissions secretaries to administrators who had to consider implications for grading these students.

What had long been established needed to be challenged: admissions and grading standards, placement, use of non-English-language materials, career guidance, and attendance. And in this challenge, I saw an opportunity too great to pass up. I volunteered to help coordinate a plan to accommodate the newcomers. Little did I know that this would be my first bona fide experience as an organizational change agent. As I look back on the 3- to 4-year period of deliberate effort, I can recognize premises, approaches, and behaviors that influence the work I do today as an organizational consultant.

In these different settings, I was struck by the discomfort that often developed among individuals and groups—administrators, faculty, staff, and students—and often led to conflict. In reflecting on communication and relationship breakdowns, I surmised, somewhat simplistically, that misperceptions, poor communication, and inflexibility were key contributing factors. When individuals and groups rallied against organizational authority, listening stopped and self-centeredness took over. Often, the parties involved shared similar concerns and goals but could not transcend appearances or group identities to find a common ground for future, mutual planning. Invariably, performance and productivity deteriorated. Although these outcomes are not surprising, I find that my interest in understanding human dynamics and believing in the possibility of change has provided me with valuable consulting experiences.

My organizational work has been strongly influenced by my fascination with culture and cultural differences and similarities. Since leaving the world of academics in the mid-1980s and becoming an organizational consultant, I have encountered many opportunities to address interpersonal relationships as they are impacted by age, gender, economics, ethnicity, sexual preference, and race. Many of the same principles I studied as a psychologist and educator apply: Adults are capable of continued learning and change. Although self-limiting beliefs and fears about "difference" and new models and practices are inevitable, I have witnessed behavior change at individual and organizational levels that is worthy of emulation.

Writing *Successful Diversity Management Initiatives* allows me to share the valuable learning of many organizations over the past 20 years. As I am a pragmatist, I designed this book to demonstrate the practical, day-to-day considerations that go into planning and managing successful diversity initiatives. This book addresses a contemporary topic, one that is complex and confusing at the same time—*diversity*. Although I had long been involved in the field of cross-cultural counseling, this terminology did not have acceptability in most business and industry settings unless it related to international exchanges. When I made calls to hospitals in the mid-1980s, I heard that cultural issues were not among employee concerns. Two years later, managers at a high-tech firm suggested that stress was impacting people relationships. Yes, there were cultural and gender differences between personnel, my contact said, but all had jobs to do and had to learn to get along with one another. One year later, I received a request to explore differences between members of a team of agency directors. "Were cultural differences getting in the way?" I was asked. There was no simple answer. In fact, once I became involved with the directors, I learned that miscommunication, work styles, and career goals were contributing to the interpersonal conflict. Factors of discipline, color, and gender were present but they were not the "real issues."

These incidents remind me of one of my fundamental beliefs: that we, as individuals and organizations, can be more successful if we address people problems head on. They don't go away on their own. Rather, festering continues and dysfunction may result, affecting key individuals and those around them.

The Framework for This Book

The steps described in this book are both practical and logical (see Figure I.1). Each chapter has its own rationale, guiding questions, and guidelines. There is a sequence implied by the organization of the chapters, but it is relative and flexible. Here I offer several observations regarding this framework. Some processes and tasks should logically precede others, but the model is also fluid, encouraging organizations to introduce particular tasks such as vision and mission setting either at the beginning, following the needs assessment, or not at all. Some may rely on the corporate or institutional statement instead. Furthermore, although this is a guide to organizational change through diversity, I propose that leaders and planners adapt the model to their own idiosyncratic needs, priorities, and business.

Throughout the book, I write primarily in the first person plural because my work typically involves a team of colleagues, many of whom have contributed by their actions to this presentation.

When I wrote my dissertation, I felt a strong need to begin with a chapter on historical perspectives. In writing this book, I have felt compelled again to describe some of the historical and sociocultural contexts that have lead to the contemporary business focus on diversity. Chapter 1, "The Domain of Diversity Management," begins with a discussion of historical and contemporary perspectives about multicultural, interracial relationships in the United States that affect the status quo of workforce diversity and organizational culture. This serves as a foundation for my conjectures about life in organizations, basic premises about diversity management, and the language that is essential to diversity work. I look at Chapters 1 and 2 as staging material for an initiative. They are about getting a sense of the domain of diversity management and its complexity. This domain has come into existence in the business world for many of the reasons articulated in the opening chapter. My conceptualization of the mind-set communicated in Chapter 1 is based on a sense of optimism, positivism, and pragmatism.

Chapter 2, "Preparing for an Initiative," is targeted to organizational leaders and planners. It essentially outlines a process to follow to get diversity initiatives off to the best start. Educational tasks are recommended to develop the grounding necessary to move forward. The second focus is on the key players and how they become the nucleus and power base. Strategies for building a sense of cohesion among these individuals are described.

Chapter 3, "Recognizing the Motivating Factors," is both educational and knowledge building. The task is to look both internally and externally to identify factors that contribute to a business rationale for a diversity initiative. Organizations emphasize the need to demonstrate the relationship between diversity and the bottom line. By identifying and clarifying motivators, an organization has a more articulate and less ambiguous business case.

The timing of vision and mission setting and committing to a diversity initiative is variable. Not all organizations would agree with me about placing this task later in the process. In Chapter 4, "Creating Vision and Mission Statements," the rationale for delaying the development of vision and mission statements is discussed. This also underscores the flexibility of the blueprint. Processes to consider when writing these statements are outlined, and examples from other organizations are also presented.

A major theme of diversity initiatives is internal knowledge building to design plans for change. Chapter 5, "Building Knowledge by Assessing Needs," is another phase in the knowledge-building process. Approaches to implementing the tasks of data gathering, the application of particular methodologies, and definition of terms relevant to this phase are discussed. Our bias is for the use of qualitative methodology. Implementation is described in depth.

Chapter 6, "Articulating Goals and Strategies," describes the details of moving the findings from the data into goal and action statements. This chapter picks up where Chapter 5 left off. Again, the sequencing of tasks is both logical and detailed. There are tasks for sorting concerns, issues, and themes; reframing themes into goal or target areas; and developing enabling strategies to support the goals. We stress that the process must be informed by the data and knowledge of the previous phases to ensure the development of a relevant strategic plan.

Implementing the strategic plan is the essence of Chapter 7, "Implementing Diversity-Related Strategies." Specific attention to factors that impact implementation such as logistics, budgets, timing, and human resources are discussed. The objective is to alert diversity planners to the complexities of implementation.

Training has been overused in the name of diversity work. In Chapter 8, "The Role of Education and Training," we propose that education and training are but one strategy of a diversity initiative. They cannot represent the essence of an initiative. Diversity training has been problematic for many reasons that we will explore in this chapter. More importantly, guidelines for the selection of diversity facilitators and trainers and for the delivery of more relevant and effective education and training interventions are proposed.

Diversity management issues, by design, are change oriented. To assess progress, change, and impact as a result of this organizational strategy, formal evaluations are recommended. In Chapter 9, "Evaluating Progress and Change," thorough attention is given to the possible approaches for measurement of change. The chapter benefited from Dr. Richard Woy's collaboration on evaluations with a specific diversity focus. Together, we have used our creative thinking to develop new, sound strategies to systematically assess change in different work environments. As with Chapter 5, on data gathering, issues of methodology, data analysis, and the role of personnel are elaborated.

In Chapter 10, "Identifying Enablers and Pitfalls for Diversity Initiatives," we give particular attention to a set of data that emerges through the life of an initiative but also from a formal evaluation process. We consider this a very valuable chapter because it can help diversity leaders and planners to anticipate strategies that can facilitate or impede their plans and work.

Evaluations typically give rise to a range of information that serves to inform goals and strategies for an initiative. Therefore, Chapter 11 is titled "Modifying Strategic Plans." Various considerations are discussed relating to how to utilize findings uncovered in ways that will further the process of the initiative.

Chapter 12, "Recognizing and Rewarding Progress," highlights a theme mentioned throughout various chapters. Our rule of thumb is that all initiatives need to be acknowledged and reinforced and that there are both public and private expressions that bring the positive attention to individuals and organizations alike.

Diversity management initiatives also contribute to understanding organization development and processes of change. In Chapter 13, "Developmental Stages of a Diversity Management Process," we describe a process that seems to capture, thematically, the essence of various phases in our blueprint. These are descriptive and not entirely linear, although some give impetus to others. For example, the *exploration* process gives an opening to *commitment*. One must also perceive these developmental-like changes as occurring within phases. The phases are exploration, commitment, experimentation, redefinition, consolidation, integration, and regeneration.

Chapter 14, "The Future of Diversity Management," provides a glimpse into the foreseeable and predictable yet chaotic world of business. We report the perspectives of organizational and diversity leaders from different organizations about the future of diversity management. Just to clue the reader in, these leaders uniformly envision diversity management as an integral part of all organizational life. They see it is an indisputable fact that must be addressed for sound business reasons.

Educational and work settings have been my primary training ground, opening my sometimes-naive eyes to realities of organizational life—the failures and the successes. My natural curiosity and optimism notwithstanding, I have a fascination with the behavior and theories of organizational life. As I observed and experienced life in these multiple settings, I always came away believing that organizational life could be better than it was if some thought and time were dedicated to creating an environment of harmony, support, and success.

Acknowledgments

Being actively engaged in fieldwork means encountering many supporters along the way. I believe most know who they are and will not be offended if they are not mentioned here. There are specific contributors, however, that I wish to acknowledge. They are Al Cordova, Martha Fields, Bill Fuller, Cleotha Jackson, Lewis Redding, Erica Rodriguez, Gail Snowden, Judy Sokol-Margolis, Fran Spinale, Barbara Stern, Rita Weathersby, Tom Webber, Robert Williams III, Barbara Wooten, and Richard Woy. Special thanks to my local Boston editor, Jenifer Snow, office assistant Mei Hung who entered one revision after another into the computer, and the Empowerment Workshops team. I have not been alone in this venture.

1

The Domain of Diversity Management

Historical and Contemporary Perspectives About Diversity

According to Peter Drucker, the preeminent management guru, "We are already deep in the new century, a century that is fundamentally different from the one we assume we live in. Things somehow don't fit . . ." (quoted in Reingold, 1990, p. 6). Diversity is nothing new. Human diversity has existed in the United States and throughout the world probably from the beginning of time. Gender differences were evident in the Garden of Eden; multilingualism emerged with the Tower of Babel. Ethnic, cultural, and racial differences were found within tribes and other groups of people across the continents before recorded history.

The history of humankind is a story of multiculturalism and diversity. It always has been and always will be. Whether we are speaking of the civilizations of the ancient Africans, Mayans, Greeks, or Egyptians; the kingdoms of Britain and Spain; or the predominantly Spanish-speaking countries of South America, all are examples of diversity. And over the years, all civilizations have included people who are different from one another by virtue of age, gender, race, sexual orientation, class, and physical ability.

Denying multiculturalism and diversity is as old as diversity itself. This denial has taken the form of holy wars, colonization of one country by another, and other movements designed to homogenize peoples. In the United States—a young country compared to other civilizations—expansion, colonization, and slavery have been among the strategies to create conformity and control, and outsiders have always been seen as a threat. It was reported that Benjamin Franklin was somewhat disturbed by the large numbers of German immigrants settling in the colonies in 1789. He proposed that the Germans be more equally distributed among the British, and that English schools be established wherever the Germans were too quickly settled to cause assimilation (Handlin, 1941).

Many other early examples of denying human diversity and perceiving it as a detriment can be found in the historical records of the U.S. educational system. The stated goals in the 1800s for newcomer children were to "domesticate them, to give them American flags, and to identify them with ourselves as one people with common interests" (Schultz, 1973, p. 259). The expectation was that persons of different nationalities and races could be melded into one.

The exception, of course, was the Africans who were brought to North and South America as slaves and were considered an economic commodity. Even as the white colonists were fighting the domination of British rule, they were establishing a new democracy that included domination along color lines. Inspiring this division was the publication of a treatise on racial classification in the late 1700s by a German anatomist and naturalist, Johann Friedrich Blumenbach. Blumenbach's original premises were that the most beautiful people came from the southern slope of the Caucasus mountains separating Russia and Georgia and that the greatest probability existed that humankind originated in this part of the world. When he developed his final typology of races in 1795, Blumenbach classified people into five groups: Caucasian, Amer, Malay, Mongoloid, and Negroid—in that order of superiority. The criteria that decided one's membership in these groups were beauty and industry (Gould, 1994). (Perhaps not coincidentally, Blumenbach's family was from the Caucasus region.)

When the *Declaration of Independence* was drafted, equality among men was rendered based on color. It can be surmised that Blumenbach's document provided a rationale for the unequal system of democracy that became the foundation for philosophical and practical thought about peoples in the United States who were not Caucasian.

E Pluribus Unum

A mere century old, this country promoted xenophobia to keep dark-skinned southern Europeans from immigrating, and nativist movements led by groups such as the American Protective Association fought to control the new immigrants who continued to arrive. These immigrants' standards of living were viewed as decidedly lower because their illiteracy rates ran high. Widespread testing by the U.S. Immigration Commission in U.S. schools (1880s-1910) yielded results to support the belief that newcomers from southern Europe were inferior to those who had previously arrived from northern Europe when officials concluded that the poor performance of non-English-speaking children reflected intellectual limitations of their parents.

With agricultural land in the United States already parceled out, immigrants with meager assets sought employment in the cities. Government reports during this time cited the high dropout rates among immigrants and their threat to the already overpopulated labor force. In efforts to contain immigrants, three states enacted compulsory education laws by 1900. Schools were seen as the means to Americanize immigrants and to prevent them from introducing unrest into the democratic government of the United States.

The melting pot and Americanization movements of the 1880s speak to an attempt to eradicate cultural and linguistic differences in the United States. Many newly immigrated families decided that speaking English alone was preferable to bilingualism, and ethnic traditions were dropped or practiced only during holidays. Efforts to Americanize immigrants have not been completely successful, however, particularly for persons who were and are visibly different from the early settlers of North America in ethnicity and race. Today, these peoples are considered the country's four major "minority" groups: Asian, African American, Latino/Hispanic, and Native American.

Another observation needs to be made about the myth of the melting pot. Politicians, educators, and other learned men historically sought to control and suppress the cultural differences introduced by newcomers, but it is easy to see that these efforts have not been successful. Cultural practices still prevail—Saint Patrick's Day parades, the celebration of Columbus Day, Chinese New Year, and Cinco de Mayo, just to name a few. International festivals, inclusive of culture-specific rituals, food, music, and other artifacts, continue to be celebrated across the country. The lessons to be learned from these experiences are important for a business debating the merits of diversity management. People are not malleable, and culture is not readily suppressed. Outsiders may adapt to satisfy expected behaviors and norms in the workplace and society, but they find means to express their individuality and cultural identity.

Diversity Prevails

So why all the excitement about diversity in the workplace if it has always been a part of our culture? A contemporary and compelling response can be found in the book *Workforce 2000* (Johnston & Packer, 1987). The publication of this report highlighted the obvious: The United States, historically a multicultural society, was acknowledging its pluralism in the workforce. Specific demographic trends would give the workplace a different look, the data indicated, and the authors predicted that white males would be a numerical minority in the future, outnumbered by white women and persons of color. The data also pointed to an increase of immigrants joining the labor force; a decrease in younger workers because of the drop in the birthrate in the past 15 to 20 years (particularly among white Americans); and changes in many industries requiring different skill levels, educational backgrounds, and work styles.

The point, of course, is not that diversity is new, but that it persists in the United States. In spite of the assimilation-only approach advocated by our country's early political leaders and educators, it appears that different models of acculturation, integration, and segregation have occurred. For example, some turn-of-the-century immigrants may argue that they had no choice but to reject their past and to "Americanize." Others (Native Americans and Mexicans in the Southwest) might assert that they were in place prior to the invasion by northern Europeans and that integration has never been a real possibility for them because of their loss of sovereignty. Yet, an objective review of the multicultural nature of the country reveals the following: (a) there has been assimilation across nationalities and races to varying degrees; (b) individuals, based on factors of education, economics, race, gender, and national heritage, choose to assimilate to different degrees; (c) some individuals who choose to assimilate may still be perceived as different from the "model American" and therefore not fit in readily; and (d) there is a dominant U.S. culture that individuals learn, desire to relate to, and at times reject.

It seems that in spite of admonitions about the harm of cultural differences, individuals and groups have found ways to participate and contribute to the global success of this multicultural nation on many levels—the economic and military among the most obvious. Business leaders can learn from past and current examples of managing a diverse workforce because diversity in the workplace is nothing new. It is the *rationale* and *planning* for change that will be the focus of the diversity management approach to be described in the next section. In the words of Peter Drucker (1993), "This is a time to *make the future*—precisely because everything is in flux. This is a time for action" (p. 16).

A Contextual Framework for Diversity Management

You can't shake hands with a closed fist.
—Indira Gandhi (quoted in Simpson, 1988, p. 5)

To promote the concept and practice of diversity management is to support a new paradigm for present and future change based on cultural relativity, open-mindedness, reciprocity, and continuous learning. U.S. businesses need a holistic vehicle to provide flexible and adaptive direction in times of uncertainty. We only need to look to the European continent to see the tragedies of not addressing human diversity. History reveals that people want to maintain their uniqueness; if people are the fabric and substance of U.S. industries, it cannot be expected that they will drop their ethnicity, gender, or intelligence at the office or factory door.

There will always be "politics of difference," however, and this has to be recognized and understood to be managed effectively and ensure that political controversies are not created to obscure realities about cultural pluralism. If we recognize and acknowledge the presence of diversity, arguments about sharing or losing power, about being "politically correct," or about quotas will not take center stage. These arguments often have been the motivating factors behind the development of organizational diversity initiatives; even more often they have been barriers to the initiative's success. Companies and institutions need to empower themselves if they choose to carry out a diversity management approach. The first step in this process is to examine some fundamental assumptions that influence organizational thinking and practices, because these in turn influence organizational leadership.

The diversity management model described in this book (see Figure I.1 in the Introduction) is based on eight basic assumptions about people, organizations, and society living in a "society of organizations" (Drucker, 1993). These assumptions are contextual and developmental, influenced by historical, political, economic, and sociocultural factors. It is helpful to look at these assumptions as complementary entities that cannot be discussed in isolation from one another or from the landscape that surrounds them. Developing an orientation toward diversity management requires understanding this framework, including the assumptions about society, organizations, and people and their dynamics and impact on businesses. Not recognizing and taking the assumptions into consideration is likely to lead to gaps and errors in organizational thinking and planning.

1. *The United States Is a Multicultural Society.* Very simply, the United States has always been a multicultural society. The arrival of the early European settlers to the East Coast and their decision to live among the Native Americans speak to the establishment of a multicultural, interracial colony. As colonizers pushed west, they encountered other Native Americans and Mexicans living in what is now the U.S.

Southwest. More interracial and intercultural relationships emerged, and with the waves of immigration from northern and southern Europe, different ethnic groups or nationalities began to impact the dominant white British, Dutch, German, and Scottish-based societies. The importation of Chinese workers on the West Coast, and persons of African heritage as slaves in the South, broadened the interracial base of the country. Multiculturalism is an inclusive term that references all societies. To limit the meaning of multiculturalism by excluding white persons of European heritage is a gross error. The same assumption can be applied to U.S. workplaces; as microsystems of the nation, they too are multicultural.

2. Each Individual Is a Cultural Entity With a Personal Culture. All individuals are born into a family system with existing beliefs, values, rules, and cultural practices. The family culture is the early shaper of a child and is influenced by societal standards, ethnic and racial identity practices, and other cultural variables. In some families, emphasis may be on education, religion, and achievement; others may stress sports, high-paying jobs, and nontraditional roles for women or men. Origins are also a factor in the development of a personal culture. Individuals who trace their heritage to ancestors who arrived on the *Mayflower* will have a different orientation to their family history and cultural heritage than immigrants who arrived in 1990, some 400 years later, or African Americans who acknowledge that their surname is that of a slave owner.

All people are impacted by surrounding events and relationships, but each of us has historic, economic, sociocultural, and sociopolitical contexts that provide a framework that further impacts our personal culture. By being born and growing up after World War II, for example, a daughter or son has sociocultural and political encounters different from parents who grew up during the Depression. It is these different and varying sets of experiences that provide individuals with a personal culture and worldview.

The Dimensions of Personal Identity model (see Figure 1.1 and Appendix A) is a summary representation of the complexity of an individual. Through the model, one can recognize the different dimensions that contribute to each individual's personal culture.

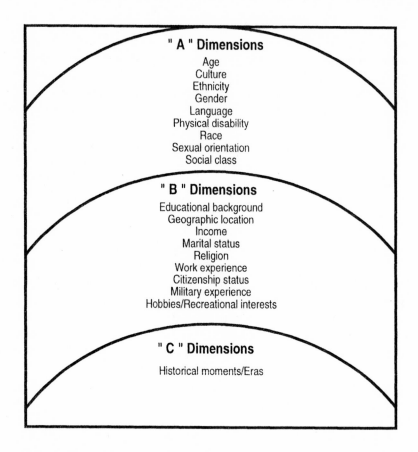

Figure 1.1. Dimensions of Personal Identity
© Empowerment Workshops, Inc.

3. All Organizations and Institutions Have a Culture. Like people, organizations have a starting point and a history, defined by the philosophy and mission of their founders. Without a doubt, the majority of these founders in the United States have been white males. Not surprising, these men have largely established hierarchical organizations that are paternal and powerful in nature. Norms and practices about dress, communication, who speaks to whom and how, salaries, and promotions are all identifiers of organizational cultural practices.

The staffing patterns we are questioning today emerged from these original models and practices: white males in management and other decision-making functions; women in support roles; and people of color and immigrants in service, factory, or other nonprofessional positions. Though changes in staffing patterns may be pointed to, this model prevails in a majority of U.S. industries and work settings (i.e., government agencies like the military, *Fortune* 500 firms, manufacturing facilities, hospitals, and schools).

According to Schneider (1987), attraction, selection, attrition (ASA) is a process that perpetuates an organization's sameness. There is a tendency to attract and select people who are like those already there. When someone is selected, who cannot fit in, that person is likely to leave, inadvertently contributing to maintenance of the status quo.

An organizational culture provides messages, both implicit and explicit, about what is "in" and what is "out." For example, in some companies ethnic and sexual jokes and gender-based salary inequity prevail. Other firms have strong and enforceable practices against sexual harassment. We have examples from settings where calendars featuring scantily clad women still exist or guest speakers casually use race- and gender-based humor. Ironically, many of these organizations have policies against sexual harassment.

Management also sends messages about the type of employee that is valued: younger versus older workers, those who relocate versus those who do not, women who delay child rearing or do not take leave time versus women who have children. I have encountered situations where verbal support for work and family balance has been offered but without a formal dependent care service or flextime possibilities.

Organizational culture, however, is not static. The Americans With Disabilities Act of 1990, for example, has required companies to make changes to accommodate physically challenged employees. Among the changes are structural alterations to buildings, revisions of job advertisements, training for hiring managers, and performance evaluations that assess skills in diversity management. The introduction of one change factor alone can impact organizational values, norms, and practices (its culture). Typically these actions on behalf of a special population can benefit the entire workforce.

4. Personal and Organizational Culture Is Fluid, Not Static. Just what does the concept of culture encompass or represent? Studies by anthropologists have yielded a range of definitions that provide meaning. Cataloging of more than 100 definitions by Kroeber and Kluckhohn (1952) led to a widely accepted comprehensive statement:

> Culture represents patterns, explicit and implicit, of and for behavior acquired and transmitted by symbols, constituting the distinctive achievement of human groups, including their embodiment in artifacts; the essential core of culture consists of traditional (i.e., historically derived and selected) ideas and especially their attached values; culture systems may, on the one hand, be considered as products of action, on the other, as conditioning elements of future action. (p. 181)

A less-technical definition provided by Sue and Sue (1990) refers to customs, values, and traditions acquired from one's environment. Culture evolves. How a group of people live is affected by new technology, economic patterns, education, and interactions with outsiders. For example, when Spanish men arrived to conquer Mexico, many stayed and married Indian women. A new culture, known as Mexican (and referred to as *mestizo*), resulted from the merging of these two cultures. In contemporary Mexican culture, or Mexican American culture, distinctions cannot easily be made between what is derived from Indian or Spanish roots, because of assimilation and acculturation processes that have evolved over centuries. One would have to refer to language, values, traditions, and artifacts to make some distinctions. Even then, distinctions are never cut and dry because of the many more factors, interactions, and events that surround groups and individuals and shape us over time. Hannerz (1992) uses the metaphor of a flowing river for the fluidity of culture: The continuous motion and dynamic means that one cannot "step into the same river twice" (p. 4). So it is with individual and group cultures: They continue to evolve based on ongoing processes that are not always readily observable.

Culture is inherent in organizations as well, and "during normal times, a leader's job is to perpetuate the culture" (Smith, 1993, p. 17). But during times of economic chaos and power shifts (Toffler, 1990), no organization is immune to culture change. Take the example of two companies that merge, each with its own culture. The merger will require two-way acculturation and accommodation. Will one culture dominate? If Company X is absorbing Company B, it is more likely that Company X's culture will dominate. When a parent company decides to consolidate by merging two of its subsidiaries, something similar may occur. The unit that is "more valued," and this will be implicitly known, will likely exercise its cultural norms and practices over the other. But the dominant organization will also absorb some of the cultural influence of the secondary organization.

Another example of change in the work culture can be seen when we consider the passage of the Civil Rights Act of 1964. By law, white women and persons of color were put on "equal" footing with white men in many domains, including housing and employment. With respect to work settings, the impact of change was felt primarily in the professional ranks. As white women and people of color were hired and promoted into management positions, different messages about cultural norms were communicated—that is, that white women and people of color can be managers just like white men.

It is simplistic to assume that significant culture change occurs through new hires and promotions. In fact, the following chapters will demonstrate that there must be an integrated, multidimensional focus on organizational culture, business systems, policies and practices, and people for us to see significant culture change. Furthermore, it will be clear that change through diversity management is a process that can be planned and managed competently.

5. Organizations and People Are in Interdependent Relationships. All institutions—banks, hospitals, schools, and baseball teams—need people to function and thrive. In ancient African, Chinese, Greek, and Mayan civilizations, businesses existed. Though lacking in what we might consider our "modern" organizational systems and technology, these were, nevertheless, businesses. And as in contemporary businesses, people were essential to their failure or success.

In the present period of technological transformations and "necessary disorganization" (Peters, 1992), the concept of interdependence takes on greater magnitude, for it is workers who must bridge the gap between the organization's changing goals and priorities and the systems and practices that will bring them to fruition.

6. Organizational Change Upsets the Dynamics of Power and Politics. Organizational culture is a very powerful and political construct. Over the years, conflicts of minor and major proportions are played out based on misunderstandings, hostile takeover attempts, and differences in business priorities. All could be termed cultural conflicts based on an upset in the equilibrium of the organization. Most of us dislike change of any type, particularly when it is perceived as imposed change. What happens, then, when diversity becomes a motivator for change?

The introduction of a diversity initiative typically generates a range of individual and group reactions within an organization. Persons who may have felt excluded from the mainstream of the organization because of their "difference" may now envision new possibilities for inclusion and perhaps even power sharing. The company's message about the domain of diversity management and its inclusiveness may reassure and encourage individuals to become more visible participants in the workforce. Not everyone, however, will have this perspective. Some may see diversity management as a threat to their power.

In the context of U.S. business, white men are reported to feel the greatest unease and resistance to an organizational diversity agenda. This reaction exists in spite of data indicating that white men continue to hold positions of power in all industries and government.

7. Organizations Operate Through Critical Business Systems, Policies, and Practices. Most organizations depend on a number of operational and performance management systems. According to human resources personnel, these represent the infrastructure of an organization and define practices that are essential to its existence. These systems typically have a formal and informal nature that influence the way business gets done and that extends to employees and customers alike.

In my work, I have identified nine major business systems and operations contributing to organizational culture that I consider critical (see Figure 1.2). These are (a) management practices; (b) communication systems; (c) work assignments and staffing; (d) career development; (e) recruitment, selection, hiring, and orientation; (f) performance management; (g) rewards and corrective action; (h) compensation and benefits; and (i) education and training.

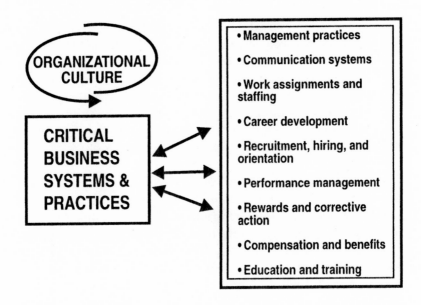

Figure 1.2. Critical Business Systems and Practices
© Empowerment Workshops, Inc.

The operative word relative to these systems is *formal*. For example, does an organization's "operational management" have a communication policy or set of guidelines? In some companies, I have found the informal grapevine to be the authentic source of information because of the absence of other functional procedures. Orientation is another practice that can facilitate the smooth adjustment of a new hire or a transfer. Again, I have often found that new employees might be assigned informally to someone to show them around but are left to discover much of what they need to know about the business on their own. A lack of consistency or absence of specificity may prevail.

What do business systems, policies, and practices have to do with diversity management? Working from the assumption that all workforces are multicultural and diverse, I have found that the concerns and issues that are typically identified by different employee groups—irrespective of gender, age, relationship status, or position—relate directly to one or another of these systems. For example, at one organization I found a range of concerns about having a career road map, comprehensive job postings, uneven distribution of workload, and too few promotions for women were attributed to sexism, "the old boy's network," double standards, and racism. On analysis of these concerns, I found that the lack of a formal career development program was a contributing factor to individuals' perceptions and experiences. In a later chapter, a more complete discussion will be made of the interface between workforce needs and preferences, business systems and practices, and the business goals of organizations.

8. *Interpersonal and Organizational Communication Are Usually Ineffective.* Just as people are essential to organizational existence, so is communication. I have decided to include this assumption about communication because it too seems to be the lifeblood of organizational functioning. Whether it is verbal (spoken or in print) or nonverbal, communication practices are strong forces in organizational life. I have declared them "usually ineffective" for several reasons: (a) employees representing different levels of work units consistently report problems that point back to dysfunctional communications on an organization-wide basis; (b) workforce members regularly describe their own communication inadequacies and their desire to have a larger repertoire of skills; and (c) communicating change tends to be top down, not face to face, and not considerate of the intended audience (Larkin & Larkin, 1994).

In reference to the new thinking and strategies introduced by diversity management, functional communications—both interpersonal and organizational—become essential.

These introductory paragraphs provide a type of inventory for business organizations. What are the assumptions and beliefs operating in an organization abut the organization, its employees, change, and its culture—all concepts that fall within the purview of discussion regarding workforce diversity? How does this thinking impact the perception of diversity management as a paradigm for organizational culture change? How does it feel to widen the diversity paradigm, to go beyond race and gender issues, and to consider the interdependency of individuals and systems as the core entity in ongoing movement toward change? There are no right or wrong answers to these questions, but how organizational leaders think about their business within the contextual framework just introduced gives direction to a diversity initiative.

A Definition of Terms

One of the fundamental barriers to diversity management is the language and terminology used by those who espouse it. These words have often been found to be prejudicial and negative. In this section, I define terms that are typically used in discussions of diversity management.

Workforce 2000 (Johnston & Packer, 1987) opened the door to the use of several new and old terms that have subsequently become catchwords for employers, board directors, vendors, and employees in almost all institutions. *Diversity, cultural diversity, multiculturalism, workforce diversity,* and *managing diversity* have become much-used terms in dialogue about the workforce. The frequent use of these words acknowledges a more-open dialogue about human differences, but far too often the terms are misassociated with affirmative action and therefore seen as connected solely to issues of white women and people of color. Communication also suffers from other unclear and inappropriate use of these terms. *Cultural diversity* and *multiculturalism* are still viewed by many as references to ethnic and racial minority persons. For some, *managing diversity* means managing the "difficult" employee—the physically challenged, open gays and lesbians, or immigrants, for example. As was discussed in the earlier section of basic assumptions, all persons and organizations have their way of seeing and making meaning. Accordingly, terms can be defined based on an individual's values, biases, and assumptions. Such predispositions shape the meaning, application, and acceptance of or resistance to these terms as they become visible descriptors of present and emerging changes in the workplace.

Workforce diversity, one of the most commonly used terms in publications, is a concept surrounded by confusion. For the purpose of this discussion, workforce diversity is an indisputable fact, a catalyst for organizational change, a composite of multicultural human resources, a business objective, and a learning opportunity (see Figure 1.3). My premise is that workforce diversity represents relationships between people and with an organization in the context of ongoing culture change.

For my discussion, *diversity* refers to individual human differences. In the context of organizational life, diversity is about individual

A multi-meaning phenomenon

Figure 1.3. Workforce Diversity
© Empowerment Workshops, Inc.

differences that can be drawn on and developed to promote the goals and practices of an organization. This definition refers to individual and group differences that contribute to distinct social identities. Nevertheless, confusion continues to exist about who is perceived as diverse. Quite often, attributions of (female) gender and (minority) race are correlated with definitions of diversity. This is inaccurate.

Within any homogeneous group, heterogeneity or diversity can also be presumed. For example, in one steel mill there are only male factory workers; to that extent they form a homogeneous group. The men vary in age, skill level, national heritage, and marital status, however, and thus they also form a diverse work group. To capture the dynamism and variability of a diverse workforce, individual characteristics need to be described in language that recognizes differences rather than creates arbitrary labels. The meaning of diversity will vary and is subject to definition within a particular organizational culture.

Multiculturalism is often interchanged with *diversity*. Multicultural-psychology specialists state that multiculturalism refers primarily to culture, ethnicity, and race (Sue, 1995; Sue, Arredondo, & McDavis,

1992). In fact, these are the categories utilized by the government, employers, market researchers, and other entities to record demographic diversity. In U.S. society, the major categories in use are Asian, African, Hispanic/Latino, Native American, and Caucasian. This practice introduces confusion, as the terms used make reference to both culture and race. This situation is most unclear with the Hispanic/Latino category. There are categories on census forms for "nonwhite" Hispanics. Very simply, *Hispanic* is not about race.

Diversity management refers to a strategic organizational approach to workforce diversity development, organizational culture change, and empowerment of the workforce. It represents a shift away from activities and assumptions defined by affirmative action to management practices that are inclusive, reflecting the workforce diversity and its potential. Ideally, it is a pragmatic approach, in which participants anticipate and plan for change, do not fear human differences or perceive them as a threat, and view the workplace as a forum for individuals' growth and change in skills and performance with direct cost benefits to the organization (see Figure 1.4).

Empowerment refers to a sense of personal power, confidence, and positive self-esteem. Empowerment involves a process of change that can be achieved in relation to specific goals (Arredondo, 1993). For example, if one wants to be a better manager, there are particular tasks that can be mastered, for example, through education in management, communication skills, diversity management, and organizational behavior. The end result may be a greater sense of confidence in fulfilling one's functions, that is, getting the best productivity from employees. Empowerment need not be seen as an all-or-nothing concept. If we work from the assumption that all persons have an innate wish for personal power, then teaching individuals how to achieve goals that contribute to a sense of personal improvement is a benefit for everyone in a diverse workforce.

With respect to diversity management, empowerment becomes a key, ongoing process. Individuals' involvement in the different tasks of a diversity initiative—giving feedback in a cultural audit, participating in a committee or training, and being the beneficiary of changes in organizational policies—can contribute to an individual's sense of empowerment. Because empowerment is a highly personal concept, individuals attribute varying meanings to it. In a work setting, for

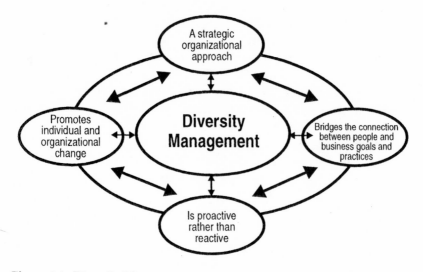

Figure 1.4. Diversity Management
© Empowerment Workshops, Inc.

example, empowerment may be seen by some as involving the relinquishing or losing of control, whereas for others it may mean long-desired inclusion in the organizational change process.

Organizational culture change is a diversity management goal that is approached through a deliberate, strategic diversity initiative. My blueprint for planning and managing diversity initiatives (see Figure I.1 in the Introduction) is a developmental model designed to promote a process of organizational culture change. In the context of diversity management, it is a long-term process designed to create a multicultural organization with an environment and practices that are more responsive to a diverse workforce and its contribution to business goals. A *diversity initiative* is the formal process for promoting organizational culture change.

Multicultural organizations are entities genuinely committed in words as well as actions to diverse representation throughout the organization at all levels (Adler, 1986; Sue, 1995). Through visionary leadership, these organizations strive to motivate and access the potential of their workforce, thereby creating an atmosphere of trust, respect, and personal responsibility. Because of their inclusionary, empowering nature, multicultural organizations can move beyond hierarchy, creating new models for work.

Diversity Management Premises, Competencies, and Practices

The core concept of this book is that diversity management is a paradigm for change with people as its focal point. To advance this paradigm, organizational leaders must have a clear understanding of the avenues that can be created to communicate these possibilities in a convincing and proactive way. In this section, I provide a more comprehensive and operational definition of diversity management. I am giving its definition so much attention because I recognize that a diversity initiative requires new and different ways of thinking about planning, and prioritizing business goals. I do not suggest that basic business concepts based on economics, forecasting, and marketing are obsolete, but rather that all of these areas need to interface with the diversity management paradigm. Basic principles of diversity management are briefly introduced below to provide the knowledge base required by leaders, diversity planners, and decision makers.

Diversity Management Is the Key to Promoting Dignity and Respect in the Workplace and a Framework for Positioning People as a Necessary Factor to Organizational Success. Diversity management will have a secure position in the realm of business management for the foreseeable future. As the diversity of people will always exist, so will the need to work with factors of change. These factors of change will be both internal and external, and domestic and international, driven by need as well as potential for emerging markets. In my work, I have found that a workplace with a humanistic culture and ambiance conveys a message of value to employees. After deliberate interventions designed to promote individual empowerment and personal value, I have recorded shifts in people's motivation, morale, and desire for improved performance. Though always considered a "soft" area, attention to the "people factor" needs to be positioned as central and key to success (Cox, 1993; De Pree, 1992; Smith, 1993; Walton, 1990).

Diversity Management Is a Strategic Organizational Goal. Diversity management interacts with all other aspects of business, that is, leadership, management practices, product development, human resources, marketing and sales, financial projections, and community and global communications. For example, let us consider two business realities: health care services have become a very competitive commodity. Organizations' marketing and sales plans are typically designed to get the consumer's attention with the expectation that people will be motivated to buy the service or goods. Cultural and linguistic considerations now weigh in as critical factors, as the following example indicates.

In several communities adjacent to Boston, there are settlements of individuals who arrived from the Soviet Union in the mid-1970s. There are different levels of acculturation and bilingualism in these communities. Recognizing a potential market, the area newspaper produces a weekly, Russian-language, 4-page insert. Health care providers communicate their message in Russian because they recognize the potential buying power of this linguistically and culturally different community. One HMO provides Russian-speaking translators and customer service personnel. This one type of diversity management activity clearly sends a message of concern and interest to a particular segment of the population. It invites persons of Russian heritage to be customers and ensures that once they are in the door, they are attended to.

Diversity Management Requires a Shift in Thinking. What is required for diversity management to be incorporated as a viable organizational strategy? The first requirement is a shift in thinking. Company leaders must engage in a reeducation process to comprehend the scope and potential of a diversity management approach. This means more than acknowledging the *Workforce 2000* (Johnston & Packer, 1987) demographics and projected trends from the 1990 census. It also means reevaluating beliefs and assumptions based on U.S. ethnocentrism— our way or no way, worldwide superiority, and white is right. In spite of the emphasis on emerging global and domestic markets as key to bottom lines, this correlation will not be realized if it is not evaluated critically alongside other data. Diversity management involves strategic thinking, leadership, and planning informed by many sources, including how to market with cultural sensitivity and appropriateness to a specific country or groups within the United States, how to recognize changing needs in developing or newly democratic societies, and how to appeal to gender differences in culturally respectful ways.

Shifts in thinking allow for simultaneous consideration of business needs that are universal or culturally relative. Seeing each individual as a "customer," whether an employee, client, vendor, or member of the board of directors, becomes a valid consideration in business planning.

Diversity Management Requires a Specific Focus on Personal and Organizational Culture, Cultural Differences, Culture Change, and Cross-Cultural Relationships Based on Interdisciplinary Knowledge. Acknowledgment and deliberate focus on culture and culture change is unavoidable when considering a diversity management strategic plan. Diversity management requires making a link between assumptions about organizational culture and personal culture (Adler, 1986; Cox, 1993; Morrison, Ruderman, & Hughes-James, 1993; Thomas, 1991). Research and open discussions will likely reveal different perspectives held about culture and culture change, but direct dialogue about culture conflicts and their consequences in the context of the work environment allow for a better-managed change process.

There are excellent publications on the subjects of management, communications, and the social sciences, including psychology, that can become diversity management tools. *Managing Cultural Differences* (Harris & Moran, 1979), *International Dimensions of Organizational Behavior* (Adler, 1986), *American Cultural Patterns* (Stewart, 1972), *Increasing Multicultural Understanding* (Locke, 1992), *Beyond Race and Gender* (Thomas, 1991), *Making Diversity Happen* (Morrison et al., 1993), and *Diversity in Organizations* (Chemers, Oskamp, & Costanzo, 1995) are a few of these. Culture change needs to be understood conceptually and practically by diversity initiative leaders because it is the key to the success or failure of communication, planning, and implementation strategies.

Diversity Management Requires Broad-Based, Relationship-Focused Thinking. Theoretically, diversity management should represent concerns and involve levels of participation throughout the entire workforce. Incidents of exclusion have been reported by many individuals seen as "different" in an organization. In diversity management, it is essential not to create new victims of exclusion. This suggests moving away from limiting diversity management to issues of white women and people of color, affirmative action, and "us versus them" tensions. Through needs assessments I have conducted, it has consistently been proven that all employees have needs to be valued and respected and goals to satisfy their personal and professional values.

In many organizations, people have complained about the white male backlash that occurs when a diversity initiative is introduced. One agency put on a training that pointed to white men as the historical culprits benefiting from others' subordination. Officials in another company were concerned about incidents of discrimination reported by individuals of color. Their subsequent intervention focused on how to improve work life for the people of color. Unfortunately, the employees' white counterparts were not included and backlash occurred.

Organizational leaders need to recognize reactions to politically fueled incidents and quickly reinforce the premise that workplace success depends on interdependent relationships. People continuously experience the "other" (Hannertz, 1992) through organizational contact. When conflicts occur, and they will, managers should use the incident or tension as a learning opportunity. The premise remains that relationships must be of a consistent and frequently positive nature among the majority of personnel to achieve desired performance and productivity.

Diversity Management Focuses on Critical Business Systems, Policies, and Practices. Assumptions about the role of critical business systems were described in an earlier section. Here, I offer a restatement to reinforce the connection between diversity management and these internal systems that are designed to support an organization's purpose and day-to-day functions. All of these systems depend on people. They are developed, managed, executed, and sometimes shut down by people. These same systems (i.e., recruitment and hiring, operational management, and compensation and benefits), however, can also adversely impact the very people who design and implement them. For example, women engineers recruited into a firm where their turnover has been consistently high suggests the lack of a receptive organizational climate that may manifest through inequitable work assignments, compensation, and rewards. Another example comes from employees who indicate that a manager's view of flextime and other policies designed to assist persons with dependant care responsibilities affects how they support those policies. There are many reports that organizations undergoing downsizing often regress to primarily male environments because women, who were last hired, are the first fired or terminated. Throughout the following chapters, there will be other examples to demonstrate the role of business systems and practices as well as organizational climate as factors in employees' sense of well-being in the workplace.

A Diversity Management Approach Promotes an Examination of the Relationship Between Systems and Practices, and People. Two lines of questioning can be addressed here: How are the diverse workforce, customer base, vendors, stockholders, and community positively or negatively impacted by existing systems and practices? How does workforce diversity support, benefit, or impede the purpose and functioning of a company?

Not long ago, I visited the diversity coordinators of an insurance company. They were concerned that their staffing patterns did not reflect the demographics of the surrounding communities. Yes, they had a recruitment strategy. They participated in college fairs and panel presentations at nearby universities and they advertised in the local papers. Their recruitment system was functional, but it still did not seem to access an *inclusive* pool of potential employees. A diversity management approach invites more questioning and analysis to elucidate why a company's hiring net is not getting a "full catch" and how there may be overlooked resources or ideas that might come from the underrepresented or "hidden" community itself. For example, what are the recruiters' assumptions about the candidates they seek? I have often found, for instance, that the term "qualified women and minorities" suggests a lesser expectation about this candidate pool. Rarely, if ever, do recruiters speak of "qualified" male candidates. What kind of pressure do human resources personnel feel? If they are instructed to hire to fill quotas, their approach is likely to have built-in biases based on negative portrayals of such hires.

Another example is based on my experience with a regional bank. Managers expressed an interest in understanding why there was such a high turnover of personnel in the sales force. Through interviews, I learned that sales personnel saw themselves as cut off from benefits perceived to be available in the rest of the company. These perceived benefits included child care networks; health club facilities; and access to job postings, career counseling, and other services that were less accessible to field-based employees. This was a diversity management issue because existing systems were not inclusive of a segment of the workforce, leaving them with concerns about opportunities and access to all the company had to offer. Inadvertently, the organization was sending a message about the lack of value of this set of employees.

Diversity Management Requires and Invites Creativity, Innovation, and Risk Taking. When a model is available, it is easier to follow the directions provided and to produce the intended product. It can be more comforting and secure to follow an existing plan, even if we are not crazy about the sample. It is another thing to create, design, and develop a new idea or product. There are no guarantees; it might or might not work.

When it comes to the domain of diversity management, the field is still wide open. There are no absolute formulas about how to do it, because what works for one company may not get off the ground at another. Peters (1992) writes about the need to "learn to love chances" as one strategy to move forward in the world of unknowns. This type of thinking is important as an initiative leader meets skeptics who may want more certainty or prefer to resist anything new (particularly something called *diversity*) that is not quantifiable. The dynamic nature of diversity management requires organizational leaders to be knowledgeable about and committed to diversity management and to anchor it to practical business goals and processes. Articulation by leadership of the connection between diversity management and organizational success is necessary for company personnel to develop and implement this initiative. Again, a clear organizational definition of diversity is a good place to start.

Risk Taking Is an Asset in Diversity Management. How is risk taking an asset in diversity management? Most people would agree that inventors, venture capitalists, race car drivers, and brain surgeons are risk takers. They become involved in undertakings that have desirable goals but no certainty. According to David Viscott, author of *Risking*

(1980), the only good risks are "safe risks"—that is, preparation and planning are essential to make risks less risky.

Diversity initiatives can be compared to an entrepreneurial business venture. An entrepreneur must follow an action plan built on sound information, clear thinking, and goal setting. One begins a business with an expected outcome or wish for success, with assurance coming from prior experience and skill. Successful entrepreneurs are not just lucky; they have taken safe risks to satisfy their objective.

Diversity management can also be a safe risk provided it is well informed. The vision from organizational leadership, tried practices in other organizations, the creative thinking of internal and external consultants, and the projection of achievable and desirable goals can inform a diversity leader. In the chapters that follow, examples demonstrate that diversity management is approachable and can be implemented with short- and long-term goals and gains that benefit the workforce, other constituencies, organizational image, and the bottom line.

Diversity Management Promotes Approaching People as Individuals Rather Than Numbers or Categories. Much of the existing literature on diversity refers to people as demographic groups—women, people of color, or physically challenged people, for example. This tendency to group has many shortcomings that I have consistently argued against. First, it subordinates individuals to a group identity that is often laden with stereotypes. These stereotypes are typically negative and demeaning, thrusting individuals into a shadow of inaccuracy.

Another problem with grouping is that it strips people of their individuality and uniqueness, contributing to anonymity and disempowerment. In the field of diversity management, this is a very risky strategy. To assume that any individual would prefer to be defined based on gender, race, sexual orientation, or any other dimension of their identity alone is a reductionist approach. Failure to see the complexity of individuals goes against the principles of leaders in many organizations who wish to create an inclusive environment that communicates value for everyone's uniqueness and difference. I have seen some negative consequences of grouping in the results of affirmative action requirements. More often than not, persons the program was intended to assist are perceived only in negative, stereotypical, or prejudicial terms. Their life experiences, including education, hobbies or recreational pursuits, or religious practices, for instance, become obscured because of one factor being used to identify them.

Grouping together individuals presumes homogeneity, and for many people talking about commonalities is safer than acknowledging differences. I sat in a meeting with a group of journal reporters and editors who were discussing the need to become more culturally sensitive. It was a fairly intellectual discussion until one reporter in total frustration broke in: "I don't know why we just don't focus on our commonalities. After all, aren't all people just people? When we cry, we all cry tears, and when we bleed, the color of blood is all the same." She was struggling to move beyond the issues of difference and prejudice and the human discomfort that they provoke; but to address only commonalities is an avoidance tactic that will likely boomerang. Human differences are present in all workplaces.

Grouping tends to create an "us versus them" image: the boys against the girls, managers controlling staff, or the doctors versus the nurses. Typically, grouping creates distance between people that is often followed by faulty assumptions. Boys keep the girls out because they see them as weak. Doctors believe they should have the last word over nurses.

On the other side of this discussion, some type of grouping is often unavoidable because of perceived and real similarities. In this book, I describe situations in which I use analogous groupings to explore perceived commonalities and differences. It has already been observed that discomfort readily arises when we come into contact with people we view as culturally different. Consequently, during our free time at work, for example, most of us engage someone who is more similar than different from us. Rather than assume this is an "us versus them" scenario, it can be considered a choice of comfort. Diversity management is about people, and people are very complex. Learning through diversity is an ongoing process.

Diversity Management Requires Visionary Leadership and Empowered Relationships. Considerable commentary has already been given to the role of organizational leadership and management in this process. My experiences also indicate that participation and modeling by knowledgeable and empowered individuals in a workplace are equally essential to a successful diversity management process. I turn to Max De Pree (1992), who eloquently asserts the role of organizational leaders: "We are not simply talking about diversity, or rights or compliance. Leaders are required to understand that this is a much deeper matter, a matter of authenticity. We are dealing with elements of human worth" (p. 57).

Successful diversity management involves a continuous learning process, one that will lead to higher quality business experiences throughout the organization. Four of the Deming management principles (Walton, 1990) support my premise: (a) institute leadership, (b) institute training, (c) drive out fear, and (d) break down barriers between staff areas. Themes of education, mutuality, and dialogue are fundamental to change through diversity.

The Blueprint

The blueprint for planning and managing successful diversity initiatives (see Figure I.1 in the Introduction) is a model that outlines the various phases, tasks, and activities that correspond to a diversity management strategic approach. Minimally, the blueprint provides an image of what a plan involves, demystifying organizational diversity work. The very design of the blueprint suggests a process of organizational change and development that is logical and practical. Because of the flexible design, I believe that the model is user friendly.

Specifics for implementation, however, still need to rely on the motivation, vision, culture, and expected outcomes of a given company. The process of thinking about and beginning a diversity management initiative requires both internal and external review. Knowledge, relevant resources, critical thinking, and imagination are essential factors in planning. These are starting points that will be elaborated in the following chapters. Today, it is possible to look to other companies and institutions who have a diversity management plan to provide benchmarks as well as lessons of experience.

Summary

Building a business rationale for establishing an organizational diversity management initiative is to be approached with thoroughness and seriousness along with a clearly articulated organizational definition of diversity. In this chapter, I have described the scope of thinking and thoroughness that must frame any and all diversity management initiatives. My intent is not to overwhelm but to provide foundational concepts and organizing principles that can lead to establishment of a multidisciplinary and knowledge-based—rather than superficial—program. I have heard too many cliches used to promote the relevance of workforce diversity to business goals. "Diversity is good for business," "Diversity will impact the bottom line," or "Without champions, diversity efforts cannot survive." Although all of these statements may be used to challenge or motivate leadership, commitment, hard work, and an orientation to continuous learning, follow through and open-mindedness are the necessary ingredients to achieve organizational success through diversity.

Guidelines and Knowledge
Base About Diversity Management

1. Diversity management must be understood in the context of historical, political, and sociocultural antecedents.
2. A planned, systematic process of change is a theme in diversity management.
3. Diversity management initiatives are integrated, multidisciplinary approaches that simultaneously address organizational culture, systems, policies, practices, and people.
4. A diversity management initiative will be shaped by the different perspectives of people and organizations and their interdependence.
5. Clear definitions and terminology can guide an initiative.
6. Diversity management requires a mind-set favorable to creativity, risk, power shifts, and change.
7. Diversity management stresses the individual in context, not an entity defined by her or his demographic categorization.

8. Underpinnings of diversity management are leadership, continuous learning, and empowerment.
9. Following the blueprint set forth in this book can lead to thriving in a multicultural organization.
10. Organizational leadership, in word and practice, is the best asset for diversity management.

APPENDIX A

Dimensions of Personal Identity

The Dimensions of Personal Identity model (Arredondo & Glauner, 1992) can be utilized as a paradigm as well as a management tool (see Figure 1.1). It provides a reference point for recognizing the complexity of all persons. The model highlights our different identity-based affiliations, memberships, and subcultures. It furthers the understanding of diversity as applying to all individuals and our performance in different environments.

A Dimensions. The A dimensions include a list of characteristics, the majority of which we are born with or into, that are unchangeable. For example, our age, gender, culture, ethnicity, race, and language are predetermined. We have no control over these when we are born and there is very little we can do to change most of these criteria. Some research suggests that sexual orientation is biologically based, although other data promote a sociocultural explanation. For some individuals, it has been possible to transcend their economic origin, but socioeconomic status based on one's culture or society may persist for generations.

Advocates of the Americans With Disabilities Act of 1990 remind the public that everyone is "one accident away from being disabled." Because the effects of an injury are usually irreversible, this is also considered an A dimension. It should be noted that two of the A characteristics—gender and race—are protected from discrimination based on Title VII of the Civil Rights Act of 1964 and that some state laws extend protection against discrimination based on sexual orientation. The other noteworthy feature of the A dimensions list is that it is about these characteristics that stereotypes, assumptions, and judgments are most quickly based on. A person speaking English with an accent, for instance, can be assessed and stereotyped in one of several ways. The accent could signal "lesser" intelligence and an individual who is more difficult to deal with; or as in the case of British and Australian accents, individuals who are highly desirable and valued.

C Dimensions. The time one is born is an historical moment that will never happen again. In presentations, I usually encourage people to think about the following questions: How was your family life at the time of your birth? What was taking place in the local community or in your home country? What was going on in the world? Reflecting on the questions and the data that emerge provides individuals with a landscape for their personal history. Persons who were born or grew up in the late 1970s and 1980s probably had greater economic and material options than those who lived in the Depression decade, for example. There is a different type of story for immigrants and refugees: The relationship between their country and the United States, their socioeconomic circumstances, and their racial heritage will all have a bearing on their status, adjustment, and acceptance in this country.

B Dimensions. The B dimensions are discussed last because they represent the "consequences" of the A and C dimensions. What occurs to individuals relative to their B dimensions is influenced by some of the immutable characteristics of the A dimensions and the major historical and political features of the C dimensions.

Educational experience is one example. Many more white women and people of color have pursued higher education in the past 20 years as opportunities and access have become more possible because of Title VII of the Civil Rights Act of 1964. As a result of this legislation, colleges and universities can no longer discriminate based on gender, race, religion, and so forth. As a result of increased levels of education, the work experience and parental status for women looks more varied than it did 25 years ago.

A more modern example can be seen in the fact that individuals who are gay or lesbian may have the possibility of self-defining even in the workplace. Again, a legal framework is loosening restrictions, taboos, and double standards.

The B dimensions also represent possible shared experiences that might not be observable by stopping with an A dimension. You cannot tell a person is from Ohio, is a single mother, or is an avid golfer by looking at her out of context. If you see a woman with a child, you might assume she is the mother, although you may not be able to discern her relationship status. Is she heterosexual or lesbian, an unmarried mother, divorced or married? There are many possibilities.

The B dimensions can be points of connections. In presentations, I usually ask about individuals' identity based on B dimensions. People from the same organization are invariably surprised when they learn others attended the same university, were also in the military, or have children under 5. There are ways that categories can actually foster interpersonal relationships rather than distance in the workplace.

A, B, C Dimension Summary. The purpose of this model is to demonstrate the complexity and variability of individuals. The model suggests that in spite of the categories we may all fit within, the combination of these affiliations is what makes everyone unique. Personal culture is made up of these different dimensions. By definition and in reality everyone is a "multicultural person."

Through a diversity management approach, individual differences are as relevant as group membership. By stepping back and using the Dimensions of Personal Identity model as objective criteria, organization leaders can more readily see the range of potential contributions *one* person can make. I draw from my experiences, values, and individuality as a woman with Mexican American heritage who grew up in Ohio, has lived in Boston nearly 25 years, has a doctorate degree in psychology, is a former university professor, is married without children, and is the owner of a management consulting business. To categorize and see me through only one or two A or B dimensions may limit the contributions I can make to your organization. The model is meant to enhance the perspective management gives its internal and external customers. These are assets and discoveries in waiting.

C H A P T E R

2

Preparing for an Initiative

❑ What is required to get the initiative off the ground?
❑ What tasks should be part of preparation?
❑ Who will manage the process? Who will do the work?
❑ What is the role of a diversity director?
❑ What is the role of consultants?

❑ Successful diversity initiatives are built on proactive leadership with a vision for diversity management, thoughtful and innovative planning by key power brokers, respect for the existing organizational culture *and* new models, and a philosophy that values people and the continuing learning process. As leaders begin to consider incorporating a diversity management strategy into their organization, they, along with senior-level professionals, must educate themselves about the process and assess their resources. Before anything is done officially, there must be a deliberate plan to build knowledge about diversity management and to engage the strongest, "most expert" internal and external personnel to manage the blueprint process. This focus will not only lead to a well-prepared start but also serve to fortify the initiative once it is under way as, assuredly, leaders and planners are met with both spirited and resistant forces. In addition, taking the time to become knowledgeable about the domain of diversity management and the experiences of other organizations often leads to a sense of empowerment and enthusiasm.

In this chapter, I describe optimal strategies for getting the initiative off the ground and propelling it into a successful future. I use the journalism tenets of *who, what, how,* and *when* to guide the discussion. Clarification and definition can begin with these guiding interrogatives, allowing each organization the opportunity to customize its preparation process accordingly (see Figure 2.1).

Who?

All initiatives involve a number of key players. These typically include the CEO or executive director, a senior management team, a diversity council or committee, a diversity director, and possibly external consultants. Not surprisingly, questions about responsibility and accountability for this new strategy can emerge early. Strategically, it is important to clarify each player's responsibilities immediately.

THE CEO/EXECUTIVE DIRECTOR

Quite often, the executive assumes the role of visible leader and spokesperson, ensuring both respect and credibility for the initiative. This individual will be expected to have final say and be the one to whom insiders and outsiders look when they want to know the organization's position on diversity. Although this executive may be only the titular head, it is still imperative that he or she be knowledgeable about diversity management as a business issue in order to communicate about it with authority and inspiration. These executives also become the initiative's role model, leading by example.

What can a diversity director or diversity committee do in case of lukewarm commitment from the chief executive? Several possibilities should be considered. First, the consultants can coach the diversity director, human resources manager, or whoever is the point person about how to engage this individual. Making the case of the "relevance" of the diversity initiative for the CEO's business direction is the

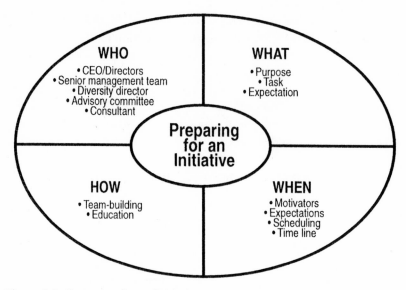

Figure 2.1. Preparing for an Initiative
© Empowerment Workshops, Inc.

starting point. Another option is for the consultants to brief the executive on the business case. Often, a presentation from an expert is compelling. The key point is to ensure that the chief executives understand the differences between diversity management and affirmative action and the rationale for positioning diversity as a business issue.

EXECUTIVE MANAGEMENT TEAM

A chief executive cannot lead alone. Many organizations have begun their preparation process by involving the most-senior or executive-level personnel. The leadership team of one health center included the medical director, the chief administrator, and the human resources director. Once this group had done its homework, it in turn involved and prepared the senior management team consisting of medical chiefs and top administrators.

The regional director of a federal agency I worked with was mandated to develop a diversity program. Her strategy was to invite the directors of training, personnel, and operations to be the planning team, empowering them to do the knowledge building and then present their recommendations to her.

The vice president of a marketing department collaborated with the director of personnel when deciding how to proceed to address immediate concerns. They had received feedback from managerial women that they would "walk" to other welcoming firms if their issues were not heard. Based on their experience and knowledge about the culture of their organization, the vice president and director of personnel immediately involved the senior managers in an information-gathering and educational process.

The common denominator among these examples is that these chief executives did not go it alone, but involved their management in the diversity initiative early on. By using this approach, executives can build a power base for diversity and also demonstrate a shared responsibility for directing change. The risk of not involving these teams can include isolation and limitations on the purview of the initiative. If individuals see diversity as only the CEO's "pet issue," its credibility will suffer.

THE DIVERSITY DIRECTOR

I have seen a diversity director appointed when I work with mid-size to large organizations. Smaller organizations may rely on individuals with a human resources or personnel assignment or someone with an administrative function to direct an initiative. Because this position will be under great scrutiny, organizations and the individuals selected to assume this role must clarify a number of points quickly. These include the following:

1. What is the source of the individual's real power? There must be a clearly outlined reporting structure, primarily one that goes directly to the top of the organization. If it does not, then the diversity director's manager must have access to the director or CEO.

2. What is the purview of the role? Diversity directors cannot be all things to all people; the scope of their work and expected outcomes must be clearly outlined in a performance plan when they are appointed and reviewed on an annual basis. This performance plan is

two-pronged, including the individual's performance and that of the initiative. I recommend this approach because the diversity director's role is to guide and facilitate the diversity initiative; he or she does not have control over specific actions. Although it is anticipated that individuals in this role will have real power to lead, to allocate resources, and to share responsibilities with other managers, they too are limited by events such as downsizing and budget shortfalls.

3. What does the diversity director offer in terms of seniority and credibility? Organizational leaders I spoke with unanimously agreed that a diversity director must have had successful experiences in the specific industry over a number of years. They must be senior-level managers, with the maturity and wisdom to manage a process of change that is often perceived and responded to negatively. Their competence in the area of diversity management will probably have been acquired through informal, experiential routes rather than through academic or formal experience, because of the newness of the field. Many have backgrounds in human resources, training, and social work. They must also possess skills in planning, conflict management, directing and delegating, and communicating effectively.

The Diversity Director Must Walk on Water. Now, if it sounds like the diversity director should possess the qualifications to be the CEO, you are not mistaken. Over the years, I have observed that persons in the role of diversity director are highly scrutinized, frequently challenged, and often unsupported. To them are attributed unenviable expectations of walking on water or of failing.

I emphasize this individual's need for executive-level skills for several reasons: (a) The position represents a cost rather than asset center, and funding it when budgets are tight can be controversial. Furthermore, the diversity director of a large organization will require support personnel. If the director must share support personnel with others, this too may be viewed negatively by peers. Some would argue that change through diversity management impacts the bottom line. But until an innovative econometrics methodology is applied, it is hard to prove this assertion and hold a diversity director solely responsible. (b) Critics of diversity and those who see other business priorities may question the need for the role and tasks. Turf battles may ensue, particularly with human resources personnel, who often perceive the purview of the diversity director as theirs. (c) Because most employees and people in general cannot distinguish between affirmative action and diversity management, they may wonder about duplication of efforts. (d) Expectations about the director are high and low. I have seen individuals assigned to multiple business committees to introduce the business of diversity, only to be relegated to the end of meeting agendas and summarily dismissed with no discussion following their presentations. Isolation often can occur, particularly if the director has no support staff or is not well received by the human resources personnel department. (e) One last related factor is the current reality of *who* tends to be in the role of diversity manager. In 95% of the organizations contacted during preparation of this book, the designee for diversity is an African American man, or woman, or a white woman. To critics, this fact often supports preconceived arguments that diversity is only for white women and persons of color. This matter is not to be minimized when we consider the overexposure often given to the role of diversity director. Therefore, it behooves the director or CEO to offer public recognition of the diversity director, acknowledging his or her previous successful work experiences and potential and ongoing contributions to the organization.

In short, the positioning of the office or role of the diversity director affects how seriously the endeavor is taken. The investment of capital and human resources must be commensurate with the support provided for managers responsible for other major initiatives.

An Insider or Outsider? One additional determination must be made regarding the role of diversity director: Should an organization appoint an insider or an outsider? As an insider, a diversity director may or may not have credibility with his or her coworkers. Based on this status, this individual will either be able to move along the initiative or will be frustrated throughout. A person with minimal credibility may be perceived as window dressing or a puppet of the CEO/executive director.

Choosing an outsider as diversity director brings both similar and different challenges. Because the field of diversity management is fairly new, an outsider is not likely to arrive with a track record of depth in this domain. In addition, the outsider will face the burden of having to fit in and prove credibility. Although most newcomers face this, diversity directors in particular report fishbowl-like experiences. They are highly scrutinized and showcased.

Guidelines for the Role of Diversity Director. The diversity director should be knowledgeable about the literature and study of diversity management. These include texts such as *Workforce 2000* (Johnston & Packer, 1987), *Workforce America* (Loden & Rosener, 1991), and *Beyond Race and Gender* (Thomas, 1991), diversity newsletters distributed nationwide, and studies being generated in the field. Participation in professional development seminars and workshops should also be demonstrated. Traveling abroad is good experience, and living abroad, primarily in a non-English-speaking region, is relevant. Bilingual skills should also be valued, particularly if they are in languages most often spoken by newcomers in the workforce. These areas of competence must be underscored: leadership, good communication, and planning skills.

My intention is not to provide a demographic profile or job description but rather to share my observations about the types of competencies that should be expected, the perceived strengths and limitations of persons in this role, and the types of challenges they can anticipate. If they recognize the tightrope-like position of the diversity director, executives and their senior managers can demonstrate greater sensitivity in the hiring and development of the individual.

DIVERSITY COMMITTEE OR COUNCIL

Here I must raise a caution: A lone individual cannot assume responsibility for an initiative. A diversity initiative is a complex and labor-intensive organizational change process. The formation of an advisory committee or council is recommended to collaborate with and support the mission of the diversity director. Ideally, this committee should be constituted by high-level individuals appointed by the CEO/executive director. I specify high level because it is through the affirmative actions of these senior personnel that the workforce and other constituencies take their cues. It should be noted here that there are likely to be other committees or task groups formed to attend to specific strategies as the initiative unfolds. This executive group need not be seen as exclusionary but rather as representing the reality of most organizations—it takes the real power brokers to move diversity initiatives forward.

In forming diversity committees, leaders must not fall into the trap of limiting appointments to women and African American men. The mind-set of the majority of Americans is that diversity equals issues between blacks and whites and men and women. Media reinforcement of this image can trickle into the workplace if there is a lack of understanding of the domain of diversity management. I encourage planners to pay attention to other constituencies represented in the organization. If there are visible cohorts of Latinos, Asians, gays, or other minority groups, they must be represented on the committee.

OTHER MODELS

For some organizations, cross-level diversity committees have proven successful and necessary. This choice is often dictated by the actual size of the organization. Larger businesses often have more latitude in recruiting or appointing committee members. For smaller businesses, particularly in the human services field, individuals already responsible for other tasks and representative of a variety of levels of personnel often make up the diversity committee. The bottom line is that real power must be given to whoever is responsible for planning and delivering an organizational diversity initiative.

Nancy Adler (1986), an international organizational strategist, defines three types of organizations: parochial, ethnocentric, and synergistic. She asserts that the type of organization will dictate its likely orientation to managing diversity, including who is involved in the development of an initiative. Not surprisingly, she suggests that the organization whose leaders believe there is more than one way to do business will approach differences more easily and to use them "to create advantages for the organization" (p. 86), whereas other types of organization will ignore diversity or try to minimize its impact. In my experience, the type of organization also influences its inclusionary or exclusionary processes when decisions about committees, diversity directors, and executive leadership involvement are made.

Considerations for the committee in performing its task should include: (a) the business of the organization; (b) the openness of the organization to past change management processes; (c) the openness of the organization to power sharing; (d) the existing management approach, participatory or autocratic; and (e) the mind-set of the CEO and senior management team about diversity management. If the latter are not convinced, their participation in the process can actually contribute to a change in their thinking about diversity.

What?

What exactly is the charge?
What is the expectation?

Clarification about the purpose of the initiative and the role of the committee and diversity director must begin in the preparation stage. What is the charge of the initiative? What is the role of its leaders? It is not unusual for diversity directors and committee members to have very disparate understandings of their purpose. Some individuals may be interested in hiring and retention goals and offering diversity training or multicultural events. Others may talk about changing the organization's culture. Some committee members may see the initiative as an affirmative action program and wonder about the duplication of efforts.

Attending to voiced and unvoiced questions about the task and responsibility can allay ambivalence and ambiguity about the initiative. Not surprising, this direction should come from the diversity director, underscoring her or his leadership from the beginning. Distinguishing the initiative from the organization's affirmative action mandate is an important first step. Often, the affirmative action officer or human resources director sits on the diversity committee, allowing him or her to provide clarification. What is required to get started, and who does it, are often the next questions. Some organizations have reported that their committee floundered for a year or more while members tried to figure out what to do.

Experience leads me to recommend that the diversity director and committee seek clarification from the CEO/executive director at the onset. This will provide initiative leaders with the business rationale behind the work they are undertaking. Without this rationale, the initiative leaders will be handcuffed. With it, they will have central reference points as the initiative unfolds. For example, one university president expressed his vision of the globalization of his school and for the preparation of students to work in an increasingly culturally diverse country. These two goals were starting points for the committee's work. They needed additional information, of course, but to begin they had to understand the president's priorities.

How?

How will a diversity director and committee members prepare themselves? To facilitate an efficient and successful working process, three strategies are suggested here: a short-term start-up plan, team building, and education. Under education is an introduction to my blueprint process.

TEAM BUILDING

As a consultant, I have learned not to assume that committee members have had prior working relationships. It is also not unusual for adversarial relations to exist among particular individuals on a diversity committee or council. There are other factors of difference that can derail a group from its charge. These include interdepartment competition, varying ideas of priority for the diversity initiative, outside organizational demands, turf issues, and self-interest. For these reasons and others, I advocate team-building activities for all members of a diversity committee. Simulations that engage committee members in experiential activities that enact and analyze teamwork may also be used.

BENEFITS OF TEAM BUILDING

Through team-building activities, a clearer understanding about individuals' self-interests, expectations, and reservations is often revealed. Interpersonal relationships that did not previously exist can be established, and guidelines for working together can be developed.

Deliberate team-building exercises can also demonstrate the need for interdependence, perspective taking, effective communication, and the ability to problem-solve as a group. How people communicate, share, disagree, and work toward a common goal become excellent learning points for the group.

Team building in one committee allowed one member to self-identify her ethnic heritage, something she had previously felt she had to hide. A white male manager said he was surprised to be invited to the committee but pleased to know that his perspectives would be heard. Members of cross-level and cross-functional groups have also reported the transfer of the team-building experience to other aspects of their work as they found themselves communicating outside of the meetings now that they knew one another.

My experiences indicate that the committee members' capacity to establish group awareness, respect, and cross-cultural flexibility sets the tone for their working process. Through these discussions, they can identify individuals' strengths, interests, biases, and connection—information that will help the group carry out its responsibilities.

The benefits of the committee, however, go beyond the individual members. Their behavior can model for the organization the reality that multicultural, cross-function teams can work together. In several workplaces, I have seen examples of this modeling. Photos of the diversity committee have been placed in the lobby of the building or other visible spots. Some companies have had photos of the committee and reports of its activities in the newsletter or a special brochure about the diversity initiative.

EDUCATION

Education is another strategy to enable a committee to work efficiently and knowledgeably. Acquiring an understanding of the domain of diversity management is essential and it can best occur through group, self-directed learning, as well as through the assistance of a consultant. Gathering information about the field of diversity management; bench-marking goals or progress through readings or discussions with people from other organizations; and building knowledge about internal demographic data and systems, policies, and practices enable all committee members to be equally informed. Informal auditing can occur through the review of previous findings of staff satisfaction surveys and of other environmental conditions identified in the diversity literature. It is also desirable for a committee to take stock of existing activities or processes in the organization that support diversity management—don't assume nothing is going on until you have checked things out.

During the education phase, the blueprint for planning and managing diversity initiatives should be introduced. Often, committees are unaware that a process exists to guide and validate their work. Discussions about the rationale for following the blueprint given the culture of the specific organization can be valuable once the initiative is formally initiated. In most workplaces, I have found that the unpredictability of a diversity initiative tends to create unease. Knowledge about the blueprint process and how it is designed to work can minimize some of the initial uncertainty and skepticism.

OUTCOMES OF TEAM BUILDING AND EDUCATION

Team building and education can give individuals the understanding and confidence to carry out their responsibility in a more informed way. Committees I have facilitated report that attending to self- and group education has minimized friction resulting from differences and priorities individuals bring to the task. Second, addressing disparate interpretations about diversity management allows for productive work to take place.

Through team-building and educational processes, committees are able to establish an organizational definition for diversity and diversity management and develop an understanding about how the blueprint for planning and managing diversity initiatives can apply in their workplace culture. Committees I have interviewed report that this awareness and knowledge enables them to communicate about the initiative more confidently and reliably to the rest of the organization. Through this process, the committee can also begin to define the scope and limitations of its role. This can be accomplished through the development of a committee mission or goal statement, one that will serve to guide their work over time.

When?

The timing of a diversity initiative will likely be determined by motivating factors (to be discussed in Chapter 3) and other organizational priorities. Direction about "starting up" needs to be determined by the executive in collaboration with the diversity committee. Individuals need to know how quickly the official initiative must begin and whether there is a projected time line, expectations about time commitment, and clarification about the interface between their committee assignment and formal job responsibilities. In other words, a strategy must guide the timing.

Another timing consideration relates to when and how often the diversity committee meets. To the extent possible, meeting times must be convenient for everyone, on a schedule agreed to in advance. Most organizations indicate that the committee's initial work requires a greater frequency of meetings to establish momentum.

Group formation, education, and development of a work plan need to occur in a timely but not rushed way. In my experience, this *formation period* takes 3 to 4 months given other work priorities. Some committees, working without an outside facilitator or consultant have taken up to a year to organize themselves. Realistically, to accommodate the objectives of team-building, education, and a preliminary, customized work plan based on the blueprint this book provides takes time and patience.

About Consultants

Questions normally arise about the involvement of outside consultants. Should it happen from the beginning, during the preparation phase, or would it be better to bring in consultants for specific tasks? There is no one right answer to this question. In my experience, the decision about whether or when to hire consultants depends on a number of factors. What is the culture and common practice of the organization? If outside consultants are commonplace, then the likelihood for their involvement is greater. How does the business value expertise? Many organizations realize that their own personnel, including the diversity director, may not be as skilled as a diversity management consultant. In this case, it would be wiser and more practical to collaborate with someone who has more specialized knowledge and experience. What is the focus of the initiative or task? Some organizations may introduce consultants to accomplish particular tasks—the audit, strategic planning, training, or team building, for example. Although this approach may seem to respond to a particular need, the use of too many different consultants may introduce discontinuity into an ongoing process. Again, thorough planning and clarification will serve to inform the best options for specific institutions. Consultants need to be perceived as collaborators and facilitators of the organization's preparation. I encourage committees and diversity directors to carefully evaluate how long they can effectively plan without one.

EXPERTISE OF CONSULTANTS

As the field of diversity management evolves, so too does the number of individuals who have became diversity consultants. There currently is no accrediting professional body to designate who can self-identify as a diversity consultant, making the issue of expertise and credibility dependent on word-of-mouth referral, impartial selection processes of an organization, name recognition, or a combination of the above. The Association for Multicultural Counseling and Development (AMCD), a national professional association, is the only association that has also developed competencies for counseling practitioners and trainers who want to claim multicultural expertise. To date, the AMCD has promulgated a set of competencies for counseling practice (Arredondo et al., 1996; Sue et al., 1992), the majority of which are applicable to diversity management consultants and trainers.

Because of the lack of professional standards for organizational consultants, questions about expertise and experience become more important. Academic credentials and degrees are not necessarily the indices to look for either. To begin with, I believe that consultants should be asked about their philosophical orientation. What is their model: adult education, person-in-context, efficacy, prejudice-reduction or any of the other foci of diversity education? Organizational planners need to determine if what a consultant offers makes sense to them.

Other criteria to take into account include the following:

1. The nature of consultation experiences and projects and whether short or long term
2. Types of organizations in which the consultant has previously worked and their possible relevance to yours
3. Formal education and work experiences in the "helping professions," including counseling, social work and clinical or counseling psychology, adult education, and organizational development
4. Formal education and work experiences in personnel, human resources, or organizational development consulting
5. Knowledge about contemporary literature about diversity management (If someone has not read *Workforce 2000,* Johnston & Packer, 1987, he or she should not be on your short list.)
6. Strong references from previous clients
7. A proven track record in previous nondiversity work experiences
8. Membership in relevant professional associations
9. Trustworthiness to share relevant organizational data

A few other considerations should be taken into account. First, try to include the CEO/executive director in the selection process. His or her knowledge and confidence in particular consultants can forge important relationships as an initiative unfolds. Second, for consultants to do their work knowledgeably, they need to be entrusted with as much organizational information as possible. Diversity management is a major organizational change strategy, and consultants must have a comprehensive picture of the past, present, and future of the business. For this reason, I stress trustworthiness of the consultants.

The worst thing an organization can do is become dependent on consultants rather than working with them in a collaborative or partnership approach. If consultants come to you as teams, this is a positive indicator. It suggests an orientation to collaboration and power sharing, and once you have hired a consultant these behaviors are a necessity.

Summary

Preparing for an initiative is a very important task. Deliberate attention to the options available to establish an initiative require education, resources, and seriousness. I stressed in Chapter 1 that diversity management is a process, not an activity or a training program. To map out a process guided by my blueprint involves dedicated time and commitment by those charged with the responsibility. In some institutions, I have seen the availability of money earmarked for diversity activities used as a hook. Money alone does not ensure an effective diversity initiative. As some of these organizations learned, launching activities without an understanding of the possibility of an overall plan and process led to complications.

I encourage "readiness," but too much of a self-directed approach can eventually lead to inefficiency. Organizational leaders must seek feedback about the progress of the initiative and offer direction as needed. Some organizations have been reluctant to engage consultants for fear of looking "bad" to outsiders. Stumbling and floundering are unnecessary, however, because appropriate consultants can facilitate the preparation of an initiative. You don't have to go it alone.

Guidelines for Preparing for the Initiative

1. Clarify who will manage the process.
2. Make the preparation phase a formal process with tasks.
3. Designate a diversity director or point person with real power.
4. Establish a diversity committee or council.
5. Clarify organizational definitions of diversity and diversity management and the purpose and expectation for the diversity initiative.
6. Conduct team-building and educational activities for the diversity committee and leaders.
7. Recognize the limitations of the committee's purview.
8. Create a mission statement for the diversity committee's charge.
9. Clarify customization and application of the blueprint for change.
10. Clarify the role of consultants.

C H A P T E R

3

Recognizing the Motivating Factors

❑ What motivates companies to make diversity a business issue?

❑ How can organizational values be a motivating factor?

❑ Will a sexual harassment lawsuit be seen as negative motivation for a diversity management initiative?

In 1956, Sputnik was launched by the Soviet Union, an event of truly global proportion. This action set into motion a competitive response from another major world power: the United States. Over the past 40 years, our country has taken pride in a number of manned and unmanned explorations in space that have included walks on the moon, the orbiting of Mars and Saturn, and launches of countless satellites. Through these missions, new information has been gathered and created, technology has been tried and advanced, failures and successes have been had, and new world order has been orchestrated. From this competitive and historically adversarial face-off between the United States and the former Soviet Union, partnerships in learning, disarmament, and peaceful coexistence have resulted.

In retrospect, it was the challenge of an external force—a major world competitor—that was one of the strongest motivating factors urging the United States to mount a strategy that would demonstrate its leadership and superiority in the space industry. Of course, there were also internal forces at play—national self-interest; fears about losing power and face in an international arena; the expectation of millions of Americans who believed we were *the* superpower; and basic values about achievement, competition, and forging new frontiers.

Earthbound Challenges of Change

An analogy can be drawn between the historical example above and the agendas of contemporary business organizations. As companies begin to consider a diversity management initiative, they need to recognize the external and internal factors that are motivating this action. What are these factors? Whenever I receive an invitation to go to a company to discuss workforce diversity, I am naturally curious about the motivation behind the call. Initial questions to company leaders include, what is motivating your interest at this time? Why do you want to do this? And most important, what are the business-related reasons?

Over the years, I have had the privilege of hearing many responses to these questions. Although no two situations are alike, my colleagues and I have found themes among the motivating forces for a diversity management strategy. The following examples are based on 15 years of experience. They have been modified to provide anonymity to the organizations.

From a financial services firm: Our account managers are young, very bright, and aggressive, but they are short on experience with clients who are different from them or the majority of their clients, such as persons of color. We've had complaints from clients about service and our employees' style of communication. Apparently, it comes across as short and condescending. Clients have also threatened to take their business elsewhere if this does not change. On the other hand, the account managers complain that these clients are too demanding and don't deserve that much attention because their portfolios aren't that complex. Senior management wants us (Human Resources) to take care of it as quickly as possible because they don't want bad press. They think some kind of diversity training will do it.

From a nursing home: The tensions between the service personnel and the professional staff are at an explosive level. Our nurses are all white women, primarily American, whereas the orderlies, nurse aides, and food service workers are persons of color, mostly from the Caribbean. Sometimes, I think it is just miscommunication because of language; people don't understand each other. We rely on teamwork, but it is not something many of our new employees can relate to. Some of the male orderlies have told me they cannot work for someone who yells at them. Apparently, the nurses think that sometimes the orderlies are being lax and yell as a way to get their attention. Some of the patients have observed this too. They said they are frightened by what they hear. It's a tight market. We cannot afford to lose patients or good employees. I think cultural differences are getting in the way.

From a manufacturing facility: Things are really pretty good here. We're a profitable company, have long-term loyal employees, and a positive image many businesses envy. In looking ahead, we have become aware of changes in the demographics of our catchment area. Over the past 20 years, families from Southeast Asia and Central America have moved in, probably attracted by the number of factories like ours. We have some employees from these countries, but they're all at the factory level. We are concerned about not having Latinos or Asians in professional and managerial roles. We know many of our employees have children who are going on to college and we would like to be attractive to them.

We also have a second problem. Because we're a manufacturing facility, our management has been almost exclusively male. We are aware that there are many women who are engineers and educated in technical skills, but we haven't done a good job of retaining them once they're hired. The feedback we get is that this is not a woman-friendly environment. So you see, we have several changes in mind, but we want to do things the right way for the future of the business.

From a nonprofit organization: We're in the people business and our image in several communities has been under fire over the past couple of years. Historically, our clients have been white, low-income families and the homebound elderly. We provide basic social services, some personal counseling, and assistance with job searches. With the downturn in the local economy, our services have been more in demand. We cannot seem to keep up with the requests for assistance and now have different types of clients. Homeless people have been using our services; gay couples and immigrant families are also new clients. Of course, our staff is not well prepared to meet the needs of such a diverse clientele. More than anything, they are feeling frustrated. Our regular clients are also upset; they complain that we're not taking care of them. We have to do something to keep everyone happy, including our funders. Some of our board members, also big donors, think we are losing our mission. Many of us are experiencing a great deal of conflict because we believe we have a moral imperative to help all types of people.

From a government agency: The federal office has made workforce diversity a priority. Now, we have to find ways to bring this to our regional offices. As you can imagine, we have a number of levels of personnel we have to reach over the next 3 years. Some won't give us the time of day; they see this as another affirmative action strategy. Others think that the government is trying to do too much for too many people and that this is the real problem. Of course, many of our employees are open-minded and want to know how to do a better job. I want to be able to convince all of them that a diversity program will help them. One of the drawbacks, of course, is that this is a mandatory program. So how do we make it appealing?

From a university: Over the years, we have offered many workshops on cultural awareness. What we have been reading about workforce diversity tells us training alone cannot bring about change. And frankly, we never thought about these workshops as serious interventions, but we also recognize that some of the problems of 15 years ago are still with us. Furthermore, other issues have come up. Here is what we face: Students of color and white women complain that their professors are insensitive and don't know how to communicate with them in the classroom; clerical and support personnel, primarily women, report that the academics are demanding and demeaning at times; the board is concerned about a decreasing student pool and the need to increase our international student enrollment; and we are receiving a lot of pressure to have a multicultural curriculum. What do you think we need to do to address all of these changes?

From a health care organization: We're a young company, still expanding. But we're not naive enough to dismiss the reality that we have a lot of competition. There is an increasing population of potential customers, but not the type we have typically served. Many are immigrants and don't speak English well and some have never received Western medical services. Our clinicians are almost 100% English speaking, so that's one barrier we have to deal with. Another new subscriber group is made up of gays and lesbians. Frankly, they make some of the clinicians uneasy, with AIDS and all that around.

Now, a second barrier we have to contend with is our board. Since the beginning, it has been made up solely of white males, as is our senior-level executive team. I am an exception as of 2 years ago. I have tried to introduce the concept of diversity to my peers, but all they are concerned about is increasing the number of subscribers. There will be an executive opening later this year and I am advocating for active recruitment of persons of color. All I get is: "We'll hire the best qualified person." What do you think will motivate this group to see more than just numbers and dollar signs, and hire people who are different from them? I know that profitability and a good fit are their answers, but there are some good business opportunities they're missing.

Identifying Motivating Factors

The vignettes above demonstrate business concerns that can be converted into diversity management opportunities. By recognizing their motivating factors, organization leaders can put an objective, business-oriented focus on their thinking about changes that may be required in the work environment. As shown in Figure 3.1, motivating factors can be categorized as external and internal.

It is apparent in the examples that motivation rarely emanates from one source. In all of the scenarios, the businesses were being challenged by multiple forces, some more manageable than others. A few may require immediate attention; others could be addressed over time. A lawsuit, for example, might be approached as a crisis and require an immediate reaction to protect the business's image, morale, or financial well-being. On the other hand, when we look at the manufacturing case cited above, we see more positive predisposing

External Factors/Motivators	*Internal Factors/Motivators*
Competition	Growth and expansion goals
Economic downturn/upturn	Organizational mission/values
Demographic changes	Organizational climate
Emerging markets	Employer/customer satisfaction
Image	Employee/management development
Investor/donor satisfaction	Continuous improvement
Government regulation	Progressive thinking
Political correctness	Profitability
Production	Performance
Profitability	Complaints
Lawsuit	

Figure 3.1. External and Internal Factors/Motivators
© Empowerment Workshops, Inc.

conditions. The company was seeking to improve its business by introducing changes. These changes are not motivated by crisis but are considered investments in the company's future well-being. The leaders I spoke with were clear about self-interest as a factor. "There's a great deal of competition for particular talent pools, but we look at it from one perspective—how this talent will contribute to our business goals. After all, there is always going to be competition," said a diversity vice president.

The case examples also demonstrate that businesses usually serve several constituencies representing different interests and priorities. At the nursing home, tensions among staff and the impact on the delivery of services were forceful reasons to invite intervention. To ignore the behavior would only allow the organizational climate to deteriorate. The director was able to articulate the connections between the business goals of the nursing home and the staff and patients who keep it in operation. By so doing, she adopted an objective perspective for promoting organizational change through diversity.

Other companies have less immediate but equally compelling motivators. The government agency discussed above received a mandate to institute a diversity management agenda. Although the motivation seemed external, in fact the local director and her managers were able to identify additional reasons that related to potential benefits for their workforce. Because they were in business to serve the public, the focus on diversity made business sense to them.

In Chapter 1, I stated that organizations and people have interdependent relationships, with business viability dependent on a workforce, membership, or client or customer base. Employees may not be the constituency that carries the most clout for any given business, however. In the human services agency discussed, for example, there was concern with board reaction to competing client needs. After all, without the board's organizational leadership and financial support, the agency might find its doors closed.

I have found in my work that responding to isolated motivating factors that occur within a business unit or department does not necessarily work, because of the interdependency of different departments or programs that are designed to contribute to the whole. Treating only one area of concern or providing an indirect response may not get to the real source of the problem. The university discussed above is a good example. There were complaints from both students and staff about insensitive treatment by professors. Cultural sensitivity training had been used over the years as a response. The complaints continued. To make change, the professors would have to be a specific focus for inquiry and intervention. Otherwise, it was likely that the status quo would remain. Stopgap measures may work for the short term, but they may not have lasting results.

The health care organization I described introduced interrelated but distinct motivators for addressing diversity. These included a lack of fit between increasing client subpopulations and clinicians, organizational leadership that seemed to focus only on the number of subscribers, and the lack of a diverse workforce. All of these factors seemed to me to be fair warnings, inviting preventative measures. At the time of my visit, however, the senior committee was not ready to pursue diversity management.

Motivators for Profit or Loss

Diversity management is never about one group of people, one type of motivating factor, or one business imperative. It is about all of these and more. The case examples we've given highlight the internal organizational goals of profitability and employee and customer satisfaction and mission, along with external factors including competition, demographic shifts, donor satisfaction, government regulations, and image. What these motivators have in common is that they all can be seen as harbingers of potential organizational viability.

If business leaders analyze the potential impact of heeding or disregarding these indicators, they might find objective business reasons to pursue diversity management. What would happen if a few customers who felt they were discriminated against by a financial services firm took their business to a competitor? In the short term, little effect might be noticed. Nevertheless, some financial loss will result and there is the long-term consideration. Most likely, these clients will not recommend the financial services firm to anyone who asks. They may, in fact, talk about it with statements that highlight discriminatory practices. A negative image about customer relationships with persons of color would mean a loss of business as well as an opportunity for competitors to capitalize on this mistake. Many institutions thrive in spite of neglecting certain customer populations, but they are bested by competitors who work to satisfy and meet the needs of all customers. In fact, well-established business writers (Peters, 1992) indicate that different markets drive industry-wide business plans, thereby requiring the focus on people as I indicated in Chapter 1.

One of the key tenets of diversity management is the power of the relationship between business goals, systems, and practices and people. The compatibility and successful functioning of this interdependent relationship impacts profitability, image, and stability in both the short and long term. The cases that I have examined all have potential for profit or loss in human and financial resources. With the evidence of motivating factors in hand, it is clear that choices about addressing change through diversity management can keep bottom lines black rather than red. The purchasing power of domestic and global markets is also a factor.

Self-Interest as a Motivator

Organization leaders who take the time to make an objective assessment of motivations for a diversity initiative are likely to identify self-interest as the most compelling reason. A short exercise is recommended to make this clear (see Table 3.1). First, list all of the concerns

TABLE 3.1 Internal and External Motivators

List all of the concerns that affect your organization, using the two categories—internal and external motivators. Take one factor at a time and assess the short- and long-term consequences of ignoring this factor.

	External Factors/Motivators Consequences				Internal Factors/Motivators Consequences	
	Short Term 1 2 3 4 *Serious None*	*Long Term* 1 2 3 4 *Serious None*			*Short Term* 1 2 3 4 *Serious None*	*Long Term* 1 2 3 4 *Serious None*
Image	1 2 3 4	1 2 3 4	Growth		1 2 3 4	1 2 3 4
Demographics	1 2 3 4	1 2 3 4	Mission/ values		1 2 3 4	1 2 3 4
Government regulations	1 2 3 4	1 2 3 4	Employee satisfaction		1 2 3 4	1 2 3 4

that affect your organization under the two categories, internal and external motivators. Next, take one factor at a time as shown in the table. What would be the short-and long-term consequences of heeding or ignoring this factor? Using the nursing home example, what would result if tensions between the nursing staff, orderlies, nurses' aides, and food service workers are not addressed? Turnover, public outbursts, patient dissatisfaction, and negative reputation are all possible consequences. They could jeopardize the quality of patient care and threaten external funding. In the short term, funding might not be impacted, but it would be over time.

For the sake of discussion, what might happen if the manufacturing company discussed above chose to ignore the changing demographics in the area and, in particular, the fact that there are now more educated women in previously nontraditional occupations such as engineering? Because the organization seemed to be one of high performance and productivity, the immediate need for change was not apparent, but if the status quo is continued another 15 years, would the company be accessible to the needs of the local community? Would women want to work there?

By making a thorough analysis of the external factors, internal concerns, and organizational goals motivating them, business leaders can more readily recognize the specific criteria that constitute their company's self-interest. In my work, I have assisted organizations with teasing out additional business themes that impact the organization's interests as a whole. These themes have included opportunities and access, fairness, empowerment, sexism or any other "ism," double standards, leadership, and management practices—their consistency or lack. I discuss these themes further in Chapters 5 and 7.

Resistance and Readiness in the Face of Motivating Factors

It is not unusual for an organization to ignore the facts and keep on going the way it was. In one of my consultancies, I encountered a CEO who decided to argue against the need for diversity management in his organization, a subsidiary of a parent firm. Although I made a logical presentation of the motivating factors and their impact on the company, he contended, "Things aren't that bad." Furthermore, he insisted on waiting to take the lead from the parent company so as not to appear out of line. With his initial cautious interest withdrawn, the planning committee's expectations dashed, and the precipitating organizational concerns still very much alive, I wondered when the crisis call might come in. Sadly, when I did receive a call, the situation had worsened. Several employees had brought complaints of racial harassment against a supervisor, asserting that he had impeded their desire for advancement. I anticipated that the environment was probably tense for many employees, not just those experiencing the harassment, and with this climate, not attending to real issues was impacting the bottom line.

Over the years, I have encountered resistance at many levels in organizations. Resistance may be fueled by fear of change in spite of compelling factors that indicate the need for change. When there are external factors such as government mandates or lawsuits, organizational leaders may resist because they feel a loss of control. Denial of wrongdoing, countersuits, and the establishment of new priorities may all follow. Some organizations report they are addressing organizational diversity through dedicated recruitment and hiring strategies and therefore a diversity initiative is unnecessary. Others indicate that diversity training is available to all employees who choose to attend. Attention is arguably being given to diversity, but both examples indicate covert resistance and an unwillingness to address systemic change. Ultimately, according to a bank executive, "There is a price to pay for not achieving diverse representation in the workforce and for not providing the accountability in the organization to ensure it."

Initial resistance may also reflect a lack of readiness to begin a process of change. This lack of readiness may be due to understaffing, production-focused lack of financial priorities, or other seemingly valid reasons. There may be a certain degree of skepticism about whether an initiative will work, and unlike other business concerns, diversity issues tend to heighten personal and professional anxieties. Discomfort about addressing human differences in the workplace is a major barrier contributing to resistance. "No one wants to think about themselves as racist or sexist, and there are a lot of perceptions because of media coverage, that this is all that diversity is about," reported a hospital administrator. "Frankly, we still tend to go home and to socialize with people who are more like us, so talking about ourselves in the workplace, particularly across our human and occupational differences, can be stressful," observed a diversity consultant.

In a widely referenced article on dealing with resistance to change, Paul R. Lawrence (1969) asserts that expectations for human change in response to external motivators become the real problem. In the area of diversity management, some of these externals include changing demographics, emphasis on social group identities to respond to marketplace needs, and competition. For a number of combined personal and organizational reasons, resistance to responding to these emerging changes manifests. Lawrence suggests that management should not perceive resistance as something to be overcome; rather they should see it as a red flag that "something is going wrong" and needs attention. Resistance is an emotional behavioral clue about how people think and feel about a particular focus of change.

With all that has been written in the past 8 to 10 years about reactions to diversity in organizations, indicators of discomfort and resistance should not be a surprise to organizational leaders and diversity committees. It is part and parcel of any change effort. In planning for the diversity initiative, apprehensions and questioning about purpose and expectations should be anticipated but not viewed as roadblocks. Rather, diversity planners must understand what motivates individuals in their organization to resist a diversity initiative. Is it a lack of good communication? Failure to use understandable terms, to connect the benefits of the initiative to the business, and to distinguish it from affirmative action can be sources of confusion and miscommunication. Another factor is management behavior. Are managers conveying an expectation that employees change but not modeling change themselves? I mention resistance at this time as a reminder to planners that the desired open-mindedness and participation by organizational members can be reinforced by clear communication from leadership about how motivators relate to diversity as a business issue.

Values as Motivators

One of the major topics that comes up when discussing diversity management is that of values. Typically, discussions focus on the values of groups such as African American or Asian Americans and how an organization may be insensitive to them. This is a valid point of consideration, but I encourage businesses instead to review the values that are fundamental to their operation, values that provide a foundation and impetus for success. In so doing, business leaders are likely to find an interface with organizational values and premises and those articulated for diversity management.

"Our mission and values statement speaks about civility and integrity and the need to put these into practice actively," voiced a diversity director. His view was that the diversity initiative provides a pathway for actualizing these principles. Another organization, in its diversity brochure, articulated the company's long-standing value statement about the importance of people. Leaders used this as the springboard and rationale for the goals of their initiative. In Chapter 4, I discuss the development of diversity-specific value and mission statements. Through my work, I have seen the strong connections to initiatives that organizational leaders can make through values-based, business language.

One source of value-related discussion is *Values Americans Live By* (Kohls, 1984). Kohls suggests that the 13 U.S. values he discusses are "judged by many of the world's citizens as negative and undesirable" (p. 2). *Control over the environment, future orientation, competition,* and *self-help* are among the values that seem to characterize the dominant thinking of U.S. organizations, according to Kohls. Yet, with the great diversity in the current workforce, it is also logical to wonder about the relevance and personal meaning of these values. Does this thinking apply only to organizational leaders or do all employees place the same importance and priority on these values? I believe the challenge is to examine these values to assess how they can be a help or hindrance in today's changing world of work.

U.S. VALUES

The following values are so often talked about when we speak of work and play (recreation, hobbies, and other leisure activities) in the United States today that highlighting them may seem redundant, but many of the clients I see have a hard time recognizing basic examples and how they influence behavior.

Competition has long been held as a unifying force in U.S. cultural history. Whether it is applied to sports, sales, beauty pageants, spelling bees, or warfare, competition is promoted as the essential factor to winning. Price wars, network ratings, and advertising campaigns all give the same message—competition is good and being Number 1 is even better. "Competition is important when it comes to the benefits of a diverse workforce. If we want to be a great place to work for all kinds of people, we have to be better than the next high-tech company. We are competing for the best and the brightest," stated a human resources director.

Individuality is a core value in the U.S. worldview. As a result, great emphasis is placed on individual self-determination and self-reliance, with each person seen as the determinator of her or his goals. In U.S. business, individuals are rewarded based on superior performance independent of those who may have contributed to their accomplishments. Through diversity management strategies and those that emanate from quality-based research, there is an emphasis on teamwork and other group efforts. This emphasis on group work can be experienced as a contradiction to individuals with a strong orientation toward individuality. Conversely, other people may be socialized in cultures that promote a more collective orientation for the common good. Women, too, have been socialized to think in terms of relationships, not necessarily dominating them but facilitating and managing them to avoid conflict. In diversity management, the focus is on interdependent relationships in the organization, still allowing possibilities for individual expression of goals, work style, and performance. Attending to the balance between individual and collective values and their expression in traditionally hierarchical organizations will become more critical.

In 1985, in an article in *American Psychologist*, Janet Spence wrote about the U.S. orientation toward *achievement.* She reported that as a society we tend to be overachievers, wanting to be first or the best at everything, leaving little if any room for failure. It is not surprising, therefore, that U.S. companies always compare in public ways their profit margins, their increase in market share, or other criteria that point to their level of achievement. Diversity management again seems to reflect this U.S. value, because another premise is of organizational success through the contributions of many. Researchers at the University of Texas reported that they found diverse work groups to be more creative and to produce "better" results in comparison to more homogeneous groups. I underscore some of the premises set forth about diversity management in Chapter 1: It leads to creativity and innovation through systematic attention to and valuing of human differences.

Pragmatism and *objectivity* are highly valued approaches to tasks in the work environment. The blueprint I set forth in this book is one diversity management example of pragmatism—following a logical, systematic plan to promote desirable, value-added change. Most business leaders pride themselves on being practical. The no-nonsense and usually less costly way of getting results or getting to a goal is most valued. A knowledge-based framework for diversity management can provide an efficient yet humanistic approach to achieving organizational goals.

The importance of being *challenged* is not often described as a U.S. value, but it does seem to be used frequently to describe many endeavors in the United States. We hear expressions about personal challenges, challenges faced by businesses and people in times of a recession, and other difficult or adversarial situations. If we refer back to the Sputnik example, we could say that the United States was challenged by the Soviet Union. When we talk about the founding of this country, we also speak about the challenges of adversity faced by the early settlers. It would seem that challenge is very descriptive of the U.S. style, a catalyst to maintain or gain power.

Contemporary business leaders and diversity planners describe the challenges associated with developing and managing a diverse workforce. "Individual differences contribute to differences in motivation for career advancement, productivity, and priorities about work and family," remarked one diversity director. Another stated that because the workplace is no longer dominated demographically by white men, a new kind of attention has to be given to the workforce and the social situations that surround workers.

Summary

Diversity management is a challenge because it introduces an unfamiliar paradigm to contemporary businesses. The paradigm promotes changes in thinking and practice that are more responsive to diversity-related business concerns. This deliberate approach can be designed to be practical, business specific, or customized and have articulated goals that are achievable. At the same time, it can be a domain for new achievements—giving one company competitive advantage in a given industry. Diversity management, with its emphasis on each individual as a cultural entity and contributor, complements the core value of individualism. One of its basic assumptions is that each employee has potential that can be exercised to benefit the organization.

Every organization strives to be "the best it can be," and if motivating factors of profit versus loss and self-interest can be recognized, this focus can take on specific forms and meaning. Finally, diversity management is a pragmatic business approach. It enables business leaders to view employees as assets that contribute to the overall success of the company, financial and otherwise.

Guidelines for Identifying Motivating Factors

1. Position organizational self-interest as a fundamental motivator.
2. Identify both internal and external motivating factors.
3. Utilize motivating factors to determine priorities for the diversity management initiative as well as short- and long-term strategies.
4. Position the organization's mission and values statement as a source of motivation.
5. Demonstrate the relationship between motivators for diversity management and business goals in general.
6. Anticipate and recognize factors and sources of resistance.

4

Creating Vision and Mission Statements

- ❑ What is a vision?
- ❑ How will a vision help a diversity initiative?
- ❑ How do vision and mission statements differ?
- ❑ Where does the business rationale fit in?
- ❑ Can a diversity initiative move forward without a vision?

The Rationale for Vision and Mission Statements

"To be, or not to be: that is the question." This often-repeated quote from *Hamlet* seems relevant to today's businesses as they attempt to redefine, refocus, restructure, merge, and maintain an economically viable presence in a rapidly changing society. When Hamlet looks into the mirror, he makes a personal challenge to himself. He raises the possibility that he could be more than and different from who he is. What might his vision be? What values, creativity, and sense of the future shape his direction? What are his guiding principles? Hamlet was a product of Shakespeare in the 16th and 17th centuries, but his exercise in self-inquiry is one heard more and more often in boardrooms, among executive directors of human services agencies, in business publications that report the decline or bankruptcy of previously successful businesses, and among employees who wonder about their future.

Today's workplace does not seem to offer the security and predictability enjoyed by our parents and grandparents. Neither does it seem to provide many individuals in our diverse workforce with the definition of an organization: "serves some human need or camaraderie, products or services, inspiration or education—through people who perform some function or work . . . a collection of human objectives, expectations and obligations" (Harris & Moran, 1979, p. 123). Like Hamlet, many people are seeking inspiration and direction, indicators that they are valued and valuable, assets and not liabilities to their organizations.

Through diversity initiatives, there has emerged a renewed emphasis on the importance of human resources and the relationship between people and the success of an organization. The blueprint in this book describes a process and set of tasks that can lead to thriving in a multicultural organization with vision and mission development as one essential element. Fundamental to arriving at a state of multicultural actualization is a shared vision.

Surprisingly, contemporary diversity management literature reports sparingly about vision setting although all diversity directors I consulted and have worked with report that it is a milestone in their initiative. "It gave our work an identity, one that became visible in various written forms like brochures, newsletters, and other artifacts," reported a diversity director in an insurance company. A hospital printed a calendar of events built around the theme of diversity that was distributed to all employees. On the calendar was the mission statement. The vice president for human resources reported that producing the statement brought people together, allowing them to practice by example, "what diversity is all about."

Example

> At the Infirmary, we value diversity of all types in our patients, as well as members of the Infirmary community. It is our goal to maximize our potential by becoming aware of and learning about different perspectives. We are the sum of our parts, and we must strive to

expand the Infirmary to reflect its culturally rich community and treat others with the same respect we demand for ourselves. By seeking the benefits of diversity and understanding differences, we will be ready to embrace challenges today and in the future.

Many organizations I have worked with have chosen to develop vision and mission statements that anchor their strategies for change. These statements catalyze the macrolevel thinking that is essential to create organizational culture change either affirming or leading to a new identity and destiny. Among the prognostications of *Workforce 2000* (Johnston & Packer, 1987), messages in *Reinventing the Corporation* (Naisbett & Aburdene, 1985), *Managing for the Future* (Drucker, 1992), and literature about business leaders as visionaries, there is one common denominator: "Strategy is only as good as the vision that guides it" (Nanus, 1992, p. 30).

The corporate mission statement often acknowledges the diversity of people, ideas, or products, but these references seldom fully express the depth needed to create direction for a diversity initiative. Why create separate statements? Some critics say it detracts from the general vision, giving an impression of self-imposed segregation. But others argue that to mention diversity in an organizational statement is merely window dressing, that there is no true commitment if diversity remains at this level of abstraction. In many settings, I have found this to be the case. The term *diversity* is used descriptively because it is a current buzzword, but often there is no substantive, concrete application that goes along with it. In my evaluation of diversity initiatives, I have found that the development and communication of a diversity vision and mission statement gives more credibility to the process. It is a "best practice."

Finally, the vision or mission statement should provide a guide for the future destiny of the organization in light of domestic and international demographic projections about emerging markets and employee pools. Visions are meant to be proactive, referring to the future as one that can be planned and guided.

Example

> We are a diverse workforce. We celebrate our similarities and differences. By reflecting the people we serve, we will achieve our personal, corporate, and community goals.

Perspectives on Vision and Mission Statements

Writers about vision share the perspective, "Vision is about leadership" (Wall, Solum, & Sobol, 1992, p. 19), involving two elements of mission statements and guiding principles. Guiding principles are sometimes referred to as core beliefs and values. Technically, an organizational vision is a statement about hope, optimism, and direction. It reflects a desired end that will foster prosperity and a long-term view for the organization. Nanus (1992) describes vision as a "mental model of a future state." As such, "it deals with a world that exists only in imagination, a world built upon plausible speculations, . . . reasonable assumptions about the future" (p. 26).

This latter statement has a direct linkage to workforce diversity. There is predictability about global trends toward multidimensional diversity, and this projected reality about the future supports the need to visualize how this diverse workforce can thrive in the 21st century. Embedded in these reasonable assumptions abut the future is the need for change in organization culture, systems, and practices.

Example

> We want to be the employer of choice by building an environment of mutual respect where all staff will be valued for who they are and what they can contribute.

Another relevant definition is that a "successful vision is based on real needs of others as they perceive them—built on common human values" (Simons, Vazquez, & Harris, 1993, pp. 88-89). Data from diversity needs assessments generally speak to this point. Findings tend to reveal that individuals, regardless of their preferred social identities of difference, want to be treated with respect and dignity. They desire personal fulfillment and a sense of recognition and appreciation beyond a paycheck. Visions allow for public statements about the interdependence of people and the viability of a business.

Examples

> The vision of HMO, Inc., is to provide an open environment of mutual respect where all staff and patients will feel valued for who they are.

> Readywear foresees global business success through the contributions of its talented and diverse workforce.

> The vision of City Human Services is to be a leader in bilingual, bicultural services that will meet the needs of our culturally diverse population.

Individuals may be surprised by the brevity of vision statements. My review has yielded more visions in fewer rather than in more words, because they are designed to cast a general perspective or intention. It is the mission statement that reflects the vision and articulates the values, purpose, and desired outcomes of an organization more descriptively. The mission is seen as providing rationale and values for action. Generally supporting the mission statement are guiding principles and core values, followed by goal statements.

Example

> St. John's Hospital should be used forever by the Sisters of Hope as a hospital, where the sick without distinction of creed, color, or nation should be received and cared for, and no patient within its walls shall be deprived of his or her ministers. We embrace the core value of respect that requires a high regard for the work of each person.

Goals:

- ❑ To create an environment at St. John's Hospital in which all members of our diverse staff can freely contribute to their full potential
- ❑ To eliminate all behavior motivated by prejudice or bias.
- ❑ To use the richness of our diversity to enhance our ability to provide quality health care in our multicultural community.

As the above example demonstrates, there is a relationship between the mission and the goals, for they inform the operations that follow (see Figure 4.1). The plan of action must be closely balanced with the mission to achieve success (Tregoe, Zimmerman, Smith, & Tobia, 1989). Mission statements begin to use enabling language about how and what actions may occur.

Example

At High-Tech, Inc., we value diversity. We are committed to creating a working environment that encourages individual initiative, respects individual differences, and values the perspective each individual possesses relative to his or her age, sex, race, creed, nationality, physical challenge, or sexual orientation. In fact, we believe that those differences uniquely contribute to a more productive and capable workforce. As a result, High-Tech, Inc., strives to attract, retain, and promote a diverse workforce of highly capable individuals.

We are committed to value and respect the strengths and differences among our customers, employees, and national communities because they reflect our continued future success. To remain business leaders in a changing world, we will become aware of and learn about different perspectives that will enhance our organizational standards, enable us to be more creative and productive, and respectfully promote domestic and global human potential.

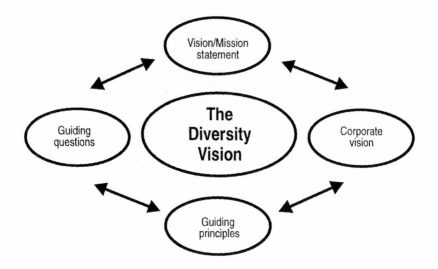

Figure 4.1. The Diversity Vision
© Empowerment Workshops, Inc.

Assumptions and Elements

In preparing an organizational diversity vision or mission statement, reasonable assumptions about the present and future need to be
made. The assumptions about diversity set forth in Chapter 1 might
be reconsidered:

- ❑ Diversity and multiculturalism are facts; they will always exist.
- ❑ The United States is a multicultural society with people embodying
  different dimensions of diversity, goals, and needs.
- ❑ The global society is both multicultural and diverse.
- ❑ All organizations have a culture that is fluid, not static.
- ❑ Organizational planning for change through diversity requires a shift in
  thinking that involves creativity, risk taking, and a focus on balancing
  individual and organizational culture.
- ❑ Diversity is a catalyst, a means to a desired end, not an end in itself.

❑ Diversity is a theme that impacts all systems and practices of an organization.

❑ Business success through diversity can be planned and directed.

Some organizations develop both a vision and mission statement, whereas others rely principally on the vision to influence goals and action. Still others invoke the corporate mission statement, relating the purpose of the diversity initiative to the corporate goals and values. Regardless of the approach or medium to include diversity in visionary thinking, there are particular elements or themes that must be captured by an effective statement.

Approaching the Creative Writing Task

CHECKPOINTS IN PLANNING A DIVERSITY VISION

The experiences of many large and small organizations and industries, ones that are for profit and not for profit alike, indicate that *planning* is a key phase in the development of a diversity vision. "You have to think clearly about what the organization intends to do about diversity. This took over a year for us," reports a diversity vice president. The feedback of many organizational diversity leaders suggests that there are particular checkpoints that can guide the process. The more detailed these are, the more likely vision writing will proceed smoothly and efficiently. All of the points support the need to work from a knowledge base, one that enables every person to be conversant about the business of the organization and how diversity management will benefit diversity directors, committees, and organization leaders. Be knowledgeable about

❑ The domain of diversity management
❑ The organizational definition of diversity
❑ The leadership for the vision
❑ The use of the diversity vision and mission
❑ The vision-defining participants and the need for representation and inclusiveness

GUIDING QUESTIONS

In developing a vision and mission statement, address the following questions:

- ❑ Who are we?
- ❑ What do we do?
- ❑ For whom do we do it?
- ❑ Why do we do it? (Wall et al., 1992)

The following paragraphs describe some criteria about the task of writing a diversity vision or mission statement. Like the checkpoints above, they can serve as guidelines and reference points.

A vision or mission statement must be believable. It is meant to communicate possibilities, but it must also be plausible. The previously stated examples were consistent with long-standing philosophies that took on a new dimension when articulated in connection with diversity and its implication for change and prosperity.

A vision or mission statement must also be aligned with a business rationale. There must be a connection to allow different stakeholders to recognize the possibilities and benefits that will accrue for the business. In some organizations, the mission and vision statement is deliberately referred to as the foundation for the business mission. With careful thinking and planning, powerful statements can result.

Vision and mission statements evolve. They generally require more than one session to complete. Remember, this is more of a process than a task. Ideas may need to incubate for days or weeks for the writers to arrive at the desirable statement. Each organization has to move according to its own pace.

The writing of a diversity vision or mission statement requires collective thinking from different levels within the organization. The vision must speak to and about all of the primary stakeholders. Diversity initiatives are about change. They open new opportunities through the language that is used and the direction that is charted.

The process involves the creativity of brainstorming and visualization. Writing a vision or mission statement involves more than facts. It requires abstract thinking, or what Jean Houston (1982) describes as "possibility thinking." Visualizations invite images of how the workplace might look in its people makeup and operations, and how this will benefit the organization. Sometimes, visualization allows an image or idea to emerge that would otherwise lie buried in hard data and numbers. For example, leaders in many organizations state they want their business to be a leader in valuing diversity through its vision. What would such a vision look like operationally in 5 to 10 years? This is what the mission statement must communicate.

Involvement of the CEO/executive director or a representative is essential—it will be viewed as symbolic of the leader's commitment to the process. In certain settings, a senior-level manager or a board member may be participants in the process.

It will be necessary to designate one or two persons to facilitate the task. The creation of a statement needs to be guided and managed to yield optimal ideas. It is one thing to brainstorm and "think big" but another to elicit a meaningful and directional statement that reflects the richness of possibilities that have been generated. Those assigned to guide this creative process should be skilled at such activities. Wall et al. (1992) provide step-by-step outlines for the development of mission statements and guiding principles.

Ultimately, experts agree that visions must be compelling, memorable, and strategic. For diversity initiatives, these criteria can empower the language and themes that underlie the statements: They are about people, products or services, and future success.

Going Public With the Vision

Several approvals will be necessary for a statement to become a public document. The number of approvals will vary based on the size of the organization, the steepness of the hierarchy, standard operating procedure for endorsement of a new organizational strategy, and the involvement of leadership up to this point. In some environments, the president or executive director may be more hands-on and prefer to move the vision forward based on his or her own initiative. The larger the organization and the layers of bureaucracy, the longer it typically takes for a vision and mission statement to become common knowledge. Leaders of the initiative, however, should not be stymied by a slow approval process. There are still other tasks that require attention.

As was indicated in an earlier chapter, planners must understand that the culture of the organization and its leadership affect how smoothly and quickly the process moves forward.

Criticism of Diversity Vision and Mission Statements

The diversity committee and vision-writing process require individuals who are committed to the agenda and willing to receive feedback and challenges they don't particularly like. They must expect criticism of the vision and mission statements. The criticism may be covert or overt, but it will be there. Through extensive preparation in planning the initiative and referring to the guidelines along the way, diversity leaders will be able to respond to criticism less defensively and with more knowledge. Well-prepared diversity committee members, diversity leaders, and even the CEO can respond with conviction and facts about the business rationale for addressing diversity management.

Critical comments about the vision or mission can be anticipated to include

- ❑ Statements are an extension or restatement of affirmative action goals.
- ❑ Statements are window dressing; companies make such statements to be politically correct.
- ❑ Putting theory into practice has benefited only those in the "Old Boy's network."
- ❑ Statements are impossible to implement; the ideas are good but too idealistic.

There will always be voices of resistance to diversity initiatives. Some may view the focus on diversity as counterculture, unnecessary, divisive, a loss of power, or criticism of the organization. For initiative leaders, this is all the more reason to be well prepared, fully informed, politically astute, and engaged with an empowered committee ready to meet multiple challenges from the beginning of the process and all along the way.

Guidelines for Developing the Diversity Vision

1. Prepare a definition of diversity and workforce diversity.
2. Understand the relationship between vision, mission statement, and business rationale.
3. Establish a clear understanding about how the vision will help the diversity initiative.
4. Ensure there is support from leadership.
5. Include a representative workforce group in the development of the vision.
6. Ensure the CEO or someone with similar authority is part of the vision setting.
7. Use a time line for completion of the vision task.
8. Be sure the committee develops a communication strategy to disseminate the vision throughout the organization.
9. Develop a vision statement that links diversity to the future direction and prosperity of the business.

5

Building Knowledge by Assessing Needs

❏ What is the benefit of a needs assessment?

❏ How will a needs assessment support a diversity initiative?

❏ What methodology should be used?

❏ Who should participate in a needs assessment?

❏ How can participants' confidentiality be ensured?

❏ What can be learned from a needs assessment?

Diversity initiatives are unique strategies because they can open the door to many unexplored and unaddressed dimensions of business goals and practice. Compiling and reporting affirmative action data to the Equal Employment Opportunity Commission (EEOC) is a readily defined numbers task, but the identification of other diversity-related matters is less straightforward. To manage change as it relates to workforce diversity, I must rely on multiple sources of data. Sound preparation, visible leadership, and motivating factors are major contributors to the organizational rationale for a diversity management initiative. As has been previously discussed, these are critical planning tasks to the direction of an initiative.

Implementing strategies for change can continue with the needs assessment phase. The guiding assumption for this task is that through assessment, knowledge about workforce diversity issues can emerge or be validated. Through the process, relevant data typically results that further clarifies and supports the direction for the diversity initiative. In this chapter, I describe several approaches and applications and provide a sampling of options in methodology. Like the previous steps, the assessment requires a strategy to guide the approach, tasks, and processes. As in other phases of the initiative, there will be variability across organizations and industries and a number of considerations to think about thoroughly to maximize the benefits of a needs assessment.

SEMANTICS

Needs assessment, diagnostics, evaluation of needs, cultural audits—all are terms that have been used, at times interchangeably, to name the task before us. I have found that the term used has to fit the culture of the organization. In health care and hospital settings, I have avoided the term *diagnostic* because it is reserved for clinical procedures. Much to my surprise, personnel for an advertising agency and bank introduced the term on their own. In my work, I typically stick with the term *needs assessment* because it seems most descriptive of the intended task.

Benefits Through Assessments

There are many benefits and positive outcomes that can accrue through the implementation of a needs assessment. Some of these potential positive outcomes can be positioned as rationale for engaging in the process. Across different organizations, the following benefits have been cited:

The Creation of an Open and Inclusive Channel for Gathering Feedback. Through an assessment, it is possible to hear from individuals who otherwise would not be called on or willingly volunteer their thoughts and opinions about workplace issues. It may also demonstrate that the organizational leadership is willing to listen to different constituencies.

Obtaining New Information About Diversity-Related Issues and Other Concerns Vital to the Well-Being of the Organization. The design of an assessment is key to the data that will be gathered, as will be discussed in a later section. The design can either broaden or limit the type of information that is sought and that emerges. For example, many organizations have approached diversity initiatives in such a way that white males do not feel included. Through an assessment inclusive of white males, it is possible to learn about their issues as one constituency in the workforce.

A second possible outcome is learning about how different elements of organizational culture and practices impact all employees. Because the workplace is a cultural context with norms and expectations for those who work there, in this process it is valuable to identify other factors in the environment that affect the well-being of a diverse workforce.

Validation of Assumptions About Workforce Diversity Issues. Sometimes, business leaders and human resources personnel have hunches about what is creating stress among employees, why performance among particular personnel is not meeting expectations, why persons of color cannot be retained as employees, and so forth. Through the assessment, assumptions can be explored with feedback either affirming or rejecting the assumptions. For example, nonmanagement personnel may report that they feel undervalued or unrecognized because they are not eligible for bonuses and do not get any feedback about the value of their contributions. Learning about this concern can better enable management to respond to one occupational group. Organizational systems for rewards and recognition may also be further explored as they relate to all employees.

Recognition That Contributions for the Diversity Management Process Can Come From Multiple Sources. The needs assessment process can be experienced as an act of empowerment. Inviting and asking for feedback, particularly from employees, can contribute to an empowerment process. Organization leaders who believe in employee empowerment can support that goal through the diversity needs assessment process.

Establishing Employees or Other Stakeholders as Sources for Problem Identification and Solutions. In all of my needs assessments, I invite employees—or whomever constitutes a relevant group—to make recommendations. How would they advise management to proceed to address the issues? The message is: Management does not have all of the answers.

Development of an Initiative Based on Fact, Not Assumptions or Political Correctness. The credibility of a diversity initiative increases with an inclusive process. The initiative will have many critics, individuals who see it as pandering to white women and persons of color, as an added task for an already burdened workforce, or as a misappropriation of monies. Leaders must clearly and openly communicate the expected benefits, financial and otherwise, for the business or organization.

A Plan of Action for the Needs Assessment Process

As in preceding phases in my blueprint, it is necessary to think about the needs assessment as a process not just a task. Working from this premise will support the development of a plan of action to carry out the assessment successfully and in a timely manner. As shown in Figure 5.1, the steps in this plan include: planning and design, data gathering, data analysis, report writing, and clarifying findings.

Planning and design is perhaps the most crucial step in the process. Organizations that do not devote sufficient time to thoughtful preparation will surely encounter other complications along the way. To avoid this, I restate a series of tasks similar to those described in Chapter 2.

Convening an Authorized Group to Plan the Process. Participants in the assessment planning process must be credible individuals authorized by the organizational leadership to proceed with the planning and implementation. The culture and usual procedures for preparing a

Figure 5.1. Needs Assessment Process
© Empowerment Workshops, Inc.

"top-driven" plan will probably dictate who will participate, but inclusiveness and representation should be considerations.

Clarifying the Planning Group's Understanding of the Process and Goals of the Assessment. An educational yet participatory approach needs to be followed. Individuals will have different expertise, interests, and priorities. It cannot be assumed that everyone assigned to the task is equally invested or fully aware of diversity management through the blueprint model. To proceed knowledgeably, I recommend the following steps: (a) team-building activities for the planning group, (b) presentations about models for diversity management and data gathering in other organizations, (c) explanations about the purpose and function of the needs assessment process as part of a comprehensive approach, and (d) assignments on a small- or whole-group basis to support the preparation process.

Articulating a Clearly Defined Purpose for the Assessment. Why is the assessment taking place? What does the organization want to learn?

Preparation of the planning group as previously described will enable the completion of this next task. The purpose for the assessment will logically be linked to the motivators, vision, and business rationale. For example, there may be concerns about a lack of women at the senior level or the participation of management versus nonmanagement personnel in companywide, community-oriented activities. Leaders in some service-oriented institutions wonder about the friendliness or openness of the organizational climate and management practices and how these may impact employees' performance and sense of commitment. These same leaders may have concerns about the effects of employee behavior and the environment on clients who seek services. In a needs assessment, statements of purpose are usually intentional, articulating goals and expected outcomes. Examples from a health care organization:

- ❑ Identify enablers and barriers to being a full contributor to the organization.
- ❑ Identify enablers and barriers to career advancement.
- ❑ Identify strengths and limitations of management practices.

Examples from a university:

- ❑ Identify factors that prevent or enable the involvement of students of color in campuswide activities.
- ❑ Identify faculty concerns in teaching international students.
- ❑ Identify factors that perpetuate classism among different constituencies of the university community.

Examples from a manufacturing facility:

- ❑ Identify enablers and barriers to women's sense of inclusion.
- ❑ Identify factors that impact effective communication among the workforce.
- ❑ Identify factors that enable or limit employees' sense of value.

The purpose for the assessment and the findings that result will · further shape the direction of the initiative. Clarification and definition of purpose must be done carefully to support the organization's vision.

Establishment of a Time Line. In one organization, I began discussions for the diversity initiative in the month of May. The leaders were clear that they wanted to carry out a needs assessment and assumed that the process could commence within 2 months. After they followed through on the steps described in the preceding two chapters and engaged in a plan of action for the needs assessment itself, 8 months had passed. The actual needs assessment task was completed successfully 9 months later. The word *successful* is used because (a) senior management approved of the plan and process; (b) attendance at interviews and focus groups reached 95%; (c) participants knew why they were in a focus group or interview; and (d) discussions were engaging, providing considerable feedback.

Timing and pacing for an undertaking such as a needs assessment will disrupt the normal course of business for individuals and organizations. One way to establish a time line and manage potential disruptions is to ask the questions, by when do we need the data? What are other competing priorities in the short term?

Setting a "drop dead" date will allow for timebound planning. For example, if the data are essential for a strategic plan that will be completed 6 months ahead, that 6-month parameter will guide the process. In addition, if the company is busy launching new products or is on a tight production schedule, consuming even more employee time, it would be important to take this fact into consideration. I recommend slower and systematic rather than rushed processes.

Design and Methodology

The majority of needs assessments I have conducted relating to workforce diversity issues have been of a qualitative nature. Because the diversity focus is on people, the assumption is that it is preferable to gather live feedback, allowing individuals to speak for themselves. A secondary approach has been quantitative. Through quantitative processes, specific data similar to those included in affirmative action reports may be gathered. Surveys and other written inventories also lend themselves to providing quantitative information. A third approach to quantifying data is based on my Critical Business Systems model. This model allows me to quantify data based on specific inci-

dents and concerns as they relate to organizational systems, procedures, and practices.

QUALITATIVE APPROACH

A qualitative approach is typically people centered. It relies on the
spoken word as the primary source of data. It involves meeting individuals in their environment or in a neutral space that provides them
with some sense of familiarity. Because it is people centered, the
qualitative approach is considered more subjective and personal. The
assumption is that by engaging participants in live discourse, the
information obtained will be more meaningful and real. "Employee
satisfaction surveys are useful, but they have many limitations. The
questions are not designed to elicit examples or explanations. People
rarely fill out the section that invites additional comments. We use
them, but find that focus groups offer more detail," reported a diversity
vice president.

The specific procedures used with this approach are the *focus group
methodology* and *interviews*. Focus groups are a qualitative form of
needs assessment, inviting participants to express perceptions, experiences, and opinions in response to a set of primarily open-ended questions. The groups comprise a sampling of the workforce according
to preestablished demographic criteria, such as African American
women, physicians, or male sales managers. Focus groups usually
involve 6 to 10 individuals for a 1- to 2-hour period. Interviews are
typically more brief, 50 to 75 minutes, and a direct reflection of the
focus group process.

Diversity planners at a financial services institution realized after
training had begun that to proceed without gathering data among
employees would jeopardize their well-intentioned initiative. They
learned through pilot training that some of the real issues had not been
anticipated and instead were being vented in the workshop. Their
decision was to schedule data gathering before proceeding any further.

QUANTITATIVE APPROACH

Quantitative approaches by definition are designed to elicit more
objective data. These typically lend themselves to statistical analysis

and can yield information in percentages or other numerical forms. In comprehensive diversity needs assessments, workforce demographics are one form of quantitative data. Surveys among different constituencies—customers, members, board members, and so on—yield information about how well the organization is reaching or serving a specific market. Checklists and other objective formats can be designed to gather quantitative information that relates to the purpose of the assessment.

Identification of Participants and Sampling Procedures. Who will be the participants and why? What is the basis for selection? There are different rules of thumb for sampling, which can vary from 10% to 20% of the total population. Oversampling may occur if there are particular constituencies in the organization who are underrepresented and so it is important to hear from as many of these individuals as possible. For example, if there are only five women in management in an entire organization, all five could be interviewed or invited to participate in the assessment. If the total population is large, randomized and stratified sampling procedures can be effective.

For data gathering, I strongly recommend homogeneous groups by gender, ethnicity, race, and occupational level. There will be some overlap in most groups based on these dimensions of identity, but the more similar the participants in a group, the greater likelihood for open and useful feedback. It is ill-advised to assign individuals with a reporting relationship to the same group.

Random sampling may yield a representative group of participants, but there are situations that do not lend themselves to this outcome. In these instances, it may be necessary to handpick some of the participants to ensure balance and representation. If through random sampling only male managers with more than 20 years of service emerge, a second process may need to occur to include less-senior managers.

The selection of participants must also reflect the purpose for the assessment. If an objective is to identify enablers and barriers to retention, gathering data across the organization to learn about different employee experiences would be the recommended approach. If a segment of the organization is omitted in the proposed assessment process, say the board of directors or volunteers, a rationale for doing so needs to be made.

Questions to Be Asked. Determination of the questions will be based on the purpose of the assessment. If one of the stated purposes is to identify barriers to advancement, the questions to ask might be, What are enablers to advancement in the organization? and What are barriers to advancement?

Do not include too many questions; usually six to eight suffice. Questions are normally open-ended, inviting discussion and anecdotal information. The recommended questions can be piloted in the planning group as a way of determining their suitability.

The sequencing of questions must also be considered. To set a positive and open tone, the initial question must be positively skewed to invite participants to give feedback based on their likes about their work or role or the organization. Questions that have been used for this purpose include, What do you like about your job? What do you like about working for Company X? What is it like to work for Company A? Invariably, both positive and critical feedback is shared.

Other questions, designed to make inquiries that reflect the purpose, are typically more pointed, as demonstrated above.

Logistics: Scheduling, Location, and Adapting to or Working Around Competing Organizational Priorities. Logistics for carrying out a needs assessment introduces inconveniences for most organizations. There will be an upset in the routine activities as employees leave their respective posts to participate in a focus group or interview. Initiative directors must coordinate with other organizational personnel to schedule dates and times for sessions. Timing and scheduling are critical factors. Ordinarily, the business of the organization dictates the best time of the year, month, day of the week, and time of day to schedule the assessment interviews. There are times to avoid such as Monday mornings and Friday afternoons, the day after a holiday weekend, and the summer months when the majority of employees are likely to take personal vacation time. Depriving employees of their lunch hour is never a good idea, nor is inviting them to attend when they have a major competing meeting. (Providing refreshments during a focus group is quite usual.)

The location or setting for focus groups and interviews must also be given consideration. Due to costs, most organizations hold the assessment on site and in an area that is comfortable and conducive to privacy. In one situation, employees indicated their discomfort because the rooms were close to administrative offices. Another group felt that the further away they were from their own work group the better. Employee opinions will vary, but ultimately settings must provide a sense of safety and openness to ensure maximum participation.

PREPARATION OF FACILITATORS AND RECORDERS

My working assumption is that outside facilitators will be used to gather data. I recommend against using internal personnel to gather feedback from other employees. It then becomes the responsibility of external consultants to identify appropriate facilitators and recorders. The facilitator has the task of directing the focus group; the recorder writes down what is said. To have the facilitator play the two roles leads to omissions. Involving a recorder means having two sets of ears in the room. I recommend against tape-recording as it tends to raise concerns about the use of the tape and other issues of confidentiality.

Preparation of facilitators and recorders is essential to ensure the most consistency possible with a highly subjective experience. Facilitators need to follow an agenda that will allow them to build rapport immediately, create a safe and open environment, and ask the prepared set of questions. Through preparation, facilitators and recorders also can anticipate problem situations, strategize about how to manage them within the organization's norms, and address issues of privacy.

To the extent possible, facilitators and recorders should be like the persons in the focus groups or interviewees. In most diversity-related assessments, some inquiries are specific to a person's gender, race, and so forth. For example, women facilitators with women's groups usually introduce a more participatory dynamic. Facilitators similar in ethnicity and race to their groups usually have very active and engaging discussions. Organizational planners must be mindful of these considerations and be assured by the consultants how these matches will be addressed.

COMMUNICATION STRATEGIES

Communication strategies are required to inform

- ❏ Organizational leaders and executives
- ❏ All constituencies and stakeholders

❑ Potential focus group participants
❑ Through written and verbal forms
❑ About the connection between the needs assessment and the overall diversity initiative

The development of a communication plan is essential for visibility and publicizing the business-related purpose to the initiative, the vision, and the needs assessment. Experience suggests that the lack of a comprehensive communication plan can create a backlash, confusion, or other negative reactions. Employees naturally want to know why they have been selected for a focus group, what is the role of senior leaders in the assessment, and how the focus on diversity will help the organization.

In *Communicating Change*, Larkin and Larkin (1994) report that communication about change efforts must come from a legitimate source. Through studies, they found that this source has a direct supervisory relationship to subordinates. In other words, the boss or CEO is not necessarily considered the best or most reliable messenger by all employees. This does not mean that the president or executive director should be omitted from the process, but simply that this person should not be the only spokesperson of record to inform the employees about the diversity needs assessment. In addition, Larkin and Larkin found that verbal communication is perceived as more accurate than written words.

The task of communication relates to informing participants as well as logistical considerations. When managers are properly informed and charged with communicating in their direct reports about the needs assessment, no one is taken by surprise. If on the other hand there is a lack of open and accurate information, managers may prevent employees from participating in a group or excuse themselves from involvement. The nature and delivery of communication about logistics for the needs assessment can be managed with ease provided all of the other bases have been touched.

Data Gathering

The implementation of the tasks described in the planning and design phase comes next. As was previously mentioned, the time and detail devoted to planning for data gathering should not be underestimated. Following my recommended outline of procedures should help to prevent any surprises.

Depending on the size of the company and other variables of organization life, information should be gathered in a very circumscribed period of time. One obvious reason is the need to control the participants' discussion of their experience, questions, or other information that might cause future attendees to be biased.

In organizations of 600 to 1,500 employees, I have carried out data gathering in one week. A business with 3,000 employees required 3 weeks' time. With a university, the schedule was made to accommodate the different constituencies I sampled. Staff and administrators were interviewed during the summer, faculty in the early fall, and students in the late fall. The board of trustees was scheduled for a focus group prior to its annual fall meeting.

Logistics are a key factor in data gathering and one I have found the most difficult to manage. Good direction from diversity planners and coordination between internal personnel and consultants can lead to smooth implementation, however.

Data Analysis

The data analysis phase of the needs assessment introduces the need for another set of tasks and skills. Not everyone is prepared for or capable of carrying out the analysis of data. Diversity directors must ensure that the data analysts are properly prepared and experienced for the job. Individuals with a background in evaluation and qualitative research, primarily from the social sciences, are usually the most qualified. In carrying out the data analysis, several processes and procedural considerations are significant.

Feedback From Individual Facilitators and Recorders. The facilitators and recorders provide two sets of eyes and ears in a focus group. Their debriefing following the interview allows for an immediate recap as well as clarification of any statements that were made. The written record jointly prepared by the facilitators and recorders will be the source of information for the data analysis.

Whole-Group Processing by Facilitators and Recorders. Following the focus group and interviews, I recommend that facilitators and recorders meet as a group to share their overall impressions in an open forum. Here, they can provide feedback about what they heard as major themes and issues and also comment about the *affect* of the groups they interviewed. Did participants speak passionately about particular issues? Were they enthusiastic about other matters?

Third-Party Review by Consultants. The next level of analysis is the most formal and comprehensive. This involves 2 to 3 consultants working together to comb through all of the data to identify themes, issues, patterns of concerns, anomalies in the feedback, and so forth. This group must be the most qualified in the analysis process as they will also be reviewing the work of the facilitators and recorders.

SYSTEMS FOR ANALYSIS

In my work, I have found that analysis can be straightforward or complex. It must follow a format or structure to provide for consistency in the analytic process, however. With qualitative data, findings are primarily deductive, as there are no hypotheses operating. The purpose and objectives for the assessment and the questions posed are key reference points in the data analysis process.

Thematic. The most common type of analysis with qualitative data is thematic analysis. In this approach, themes emerge that encompass issues and normally reflect the organization's culture. They may include good employee benefits, ineffective performance evaluation processes, or sexism. In thematic analysis, the goal is to identify recurring references to particular topics. The more often these references are mentioned across interviews, the more likely they will begin to register as a theme.

Critical Business Systems. A structure that can be employed to complement the thematic approach is based on critical business systems (CBS). Described in Chapter 1, these systems include internal dimensions of an organization that exist for employees, such as career development, compensations and benefits, performance evaluations, communications, management practices, rewards and corrective systems, and education and training. In my work, the use of the CBS format has served two purposes. It has contributed to highlighting themes that relate to specific systems and across all of the systems, allowing for quantification.

For example, using the CBS format with one organization, I found that concerns about performance evaluations emerged in the all of the focus groups. This repetition made performance evaluations a theme. Moreover, I noted the number of times they were mentioned within a group. In some groups, everyone had something to say about performance evaluations; from a quantitative perspective, statements about performance evaluations were made 10 to 15 times. If I added up the number of times such comments were made across all groups, the frequency jumped to 50 to 60. In some organizations, quantification is valued over the qualitative themes alone. Thus, it is a reasonable system to employ in particular settings.

By Work Group, Gender, Ethnicity, Race, Age, and So Forth. Focus groups based on gender, ethnicity, or some other dimension related to social identity offer another approach to data analysis. What are the concerns most often mentioned by women in general? By African American employees? By clerical personnel? By managers? It may be that issues raised by women in general do not emerge at all with men or that concerns of clerical staff are more similar to than different from those of their supervisors. Through this type of analysis, organization leaders can learn about specific needs and issues of particular constituencies and influence the action strategies that are taken.

Report Writing

It goes without saying that the findings of the needs assessment must be documented through a formal report. Those who have written a thesis or dissertation will recognize the format or outline to follow. It is important to take into account the audience and context for the report, however. In academic environments, well-documented and cited presentations are typically preferred, whereas in businesses focused on the bottom line, findings rather than the details will be given the most attention.

In the executive summary of a report, the highlights can be stated succinctly. The facts are communicated in a few pages for executives who have little time to spare. This in no way is to suggest that the summary is all they will read. In my experience, most organizational leaders read the report in its entirety, because they are curious about sentiments expressed by participants. The report provides a glimpse into organizational life as perceived by a representative sample. Anecdotes and quotes may be included provided confidentiality is not violated.

Clarification of Findings

Part of the process of reporting the findings is a step of *clarification.* This can happen in one of several ways.

Group Process for Validating the Feedback. (a) A group of employees who participated in the needs assessment can be reconvened to verify and clarify the findings. (b) A group of employees who did not participate in the assessment can meet for a reality check—that is, they can verify, disagree with, or add to the findings. (c) A group of combined employees can meet to carry out the task.

Reviewing the Findings in Reference to the Stated Purpose of the Assessment. Review can occur during the report-writing phase. As the analysts review findings and draw conclusions, they will need to cross-reference the findings to the stated purposes of the assessment. Did the assessment process provide information that was being sought? Did the findings correspond to the areas of inquiry or were they of an entirely different nature? Findings will of course be reported in the "Conclusions" section of the report.

Evaluation of the Needs Assessment Findings

The completed needs assessment is turned over to the diversity initiative committee or whoever is charged with guiding the process of the initiative. According to my blueprint, clarification and evaluation should occur at the end of each major step or phase. At this juncture, the following questions can be asked:

- ❑ What do the data tell us?
- ❑ What do the data mean in light of the vision, mission, and business rationale for the diversity initiative?
- ❑ What directions and priorities are indicated?

The responses to these questions will become the key to planning the next steps and will be necessary in the communication process that describes the assessment process itself (see Figure 5.2).

Communication of Findings—Communicating Change

All phases of a diversity initiative require continuous communication across all levels of the organization. Communication about the needs assessment findings should be guided by the following criteria: timeliness, succinctness, clarity, and openness. Focus group participants will be particularly keen on hearing the findings. But in general, the entire organization must be briefed on the findings by managers or supervisors.

This reporting process must first and foremost be verbal and face to face. The "messengers" should be thoroughly prepared to present the findings and describe the next steps to be taken as well as be able to address any questions that may emerge. These individuals are key because they add their credibility to the process and will be seen as spokespersons for the initiative as well. These managers and supervisors must work from written and verbal scripts, ensuring a consistent message.

Role of Senior Management. In the communication process, senior managers must play a role, but as I indicated above, theirs cannot be

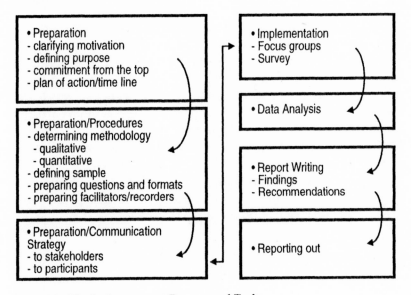

Figure 5.2. Needs Assessment Process and Tasks
© Empowerment Workshops, Inc.

the only voices heard. Logically, the CEO or president must initiate the communication process with his or her own direct reports. Following this model, however, other levels in the organization carry out the communication task. This means the involvement of managers and supervisors, or what are described in other organizations as middle managers.

Nonemployee Constituencies. Communication to nonemployee constituencies must be another consideration. The board of directors, advisory committees, volunteers, or other organized entities related to the organization must be included in the process.

Linking Findings to Strategic Business Plans

Once the findings of a needs assessment are in hand, there are several options available. The first is to design a strategic plan specific to the diversity initiative that will have a life of its own. The second is for the data to inform a larger organizational strategic plan. In my experience, both approaches work. Again, timing is important. Findings cannot sit on a shelf, because the credibility of the work will suffer and employees will come to believe their concerns were not heard or taken seriously. In one organization, findings were not reported until 2 years after the focus groups took place. Employees, both participants and nonparticipants, were critical. They wondered why it took so long, whether the company had something to hide, and how serious the initiative could be if so much time was allowed to elapse.

In the communication process, leaders should be able to share the implications of the findings and some of the next steps that will be taken. The more concrete and time specific the steps, the better.

Summary

The needs assessment is a major phase in a diversity initiative, providing a more person-centered explication of organizational issues. When an assessment or audit occurs, even the most cynical employees are affected. For assessments serve multiple purposes. In addition to fulfilling the goal of gathering data, they are an "intervention," interrupting the normal flow of business and raising questions not often discussed openly. '

Planners need to keep in mind that the assessment is designed to build knowledge, gathering data from key sources to identify organizational strengths and concerns. If communication occurs in this straightforward manner, people in general will likely be less confused. This does not mean that resistance or other obstacles will not occur. For example, an individual in one focus group made snide remarks about "the value of slavery." Another person challenged the facilitator about the company's motivation: "Who are they trying to placate?"

Generally speaking, however, needs assessment processes that are carefully planned bring positive attention to the initiative. They engage individuals in sharing their point of view about issues that matter to them, not a common occurrence in many organizations. Most assessments also invite participants to offer their ideas and recommendations about how to address concerns. This, too, does not frequently happen.

Data gathering is an important milestone in the diversity management development process. It is about building "local" knowledge. For organizational leaders and planners, the findings from a needs assessment will fortify the work of the initiative and provide the organization with many important lessons.

Guidelines for the Needs Assessment Process

1. Clearly articulate motivating factors for the needs assessment.
2. Have a defined purpose and guiding questions for the assessment.
3. Develop a comprehensive plan of action for the assessment.
4. Ensure involvement and commitment from critical stakeholders.
5. Employ multiple communication strategies.
6. Use inclusive sampling procedures.
7. Understand how data will be used and plan to link diversity needs assessment data to other strategic business objectives.
8. Use a time line to chart the process.
9. Give attention to logistics.
10. Be prepared to respond to highly critical feedback.
11. Involve highly skilled consultants in the data gathering.

6

Articulating Goals and Strategies

❑ What will happen to all of the data from the needs assessment?
❑ How can it be sorted?
❑ How can themes and issues be formulated into goals?
❑ Is a strategic plan for diversity necessary?
❑ How can accountability be built into a plan?

❑ By design, my blueprint is developmental and flexible, involving continuous planning, clarification, and implementation processes. With the completion of data gathering and the accumulation of different sets of data, the next logical phase involves utilizing the findings and recommendations for strategic planning. The development of a plan is another milestone in an organization's diversity initiative. In my nuts-and-bolts approach to planning successful diversity initiatives, I see the strategic plan as the document that can reflect the goals and actions that will respond to concerns and recommendations that emerge from needs assessments and other relevant sources.

Here, I discuss several topics and tasks: a framework for sorting and organizing findings and recommendations from the data; development of goals and enabling strategies; procedural and business guidelines for writing the strategic plan; and enablers of the process. Examples offered throughout the book come from different industries and organizations varying in size. The bottom line in all cases is that these fundamental principles can be applied when customizing an organizational strategy.

Is a Strategic Plan Necessary?

"We decided to drive the initiative through business lines such as legal, small business, product development, etcetera. We took the main issues that emerged from the needs assessment and asked each department to develop a plan to address them. This made the process inclusive but also gave broader exposure about the diversity goals throughout the bank," reported a bank vice-president.

"The museum's plan applies to everyone, from staff to trustees. The major issues have required action responses from the appropriate parties and accountability is built in as well. We have been successful because we have looked at the interconnections among people, systems, and functions—these have to support the museum's goals. Diversity plans naturally support the larger organizational vision," stated a museum director for human resources.

It is not unusual to question the necessity for a diversity strategic plan. In some settings, it is viewed as vital to the lifeblood of the organization's diversity agenda. To not have a strategic plan may be perceived as giving less value to the initiative itself. Diversity directors indicate that a diversity-focused plan is consistent with an organization's approach to a new business thrust or product. Such initiatives must have clear goals and objectives and enabling strategies that include sound leadership and management, resources, communication systems, and measurement. The success of an initiative depends on the deliberateness of a combination of factors.

Writing a strategic plan is analogous to writing a will; in other words, a legacy is being created. With diversity initiatives, strategic plans can articulate a legacy for the organization as well as set directions for accountability. As Figure 6.1 indicates, the plan is shaped by data from different sources.

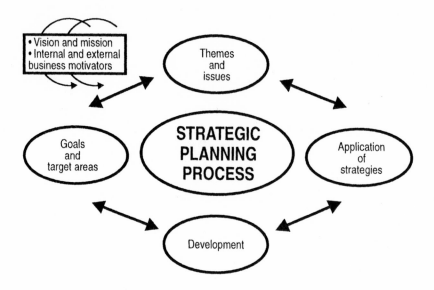

Figure 6.1. Strategic Planning Process
© Empowerment Workshops, Inc.

Some institutions position diversity management goals throughout the organizational master plan, articulating linkages between diversity and marketing, advertising, communications, human resources, and so on. Another approach is to identify diversity management as one business objective within specific departments or business units, that is, product development, customer service, or community relations. A third alternative is to integrate diversity management goals into the human resources domain. Because diversity introduces a focus on people issues in relation to a number of organizational systems and practices, it is often assumed that expertise from the human resources department is best suited to facilitate diversity management implementation plans.

There are no right or wrong approaches. As the examples suggest, the development of a strategic plan depends on the organizational culture and how leaders would like to address diversity management—on macro or micro levels.

Sorting Through the Findings

To begin the task of goal and strategy development, a first step requires a re-review of the findings and recommendations from the needs assessment. The sorting task typically involves a diversity committee, human resources personnel, or other relevant employee representatives. In this phase of clarification, it is important to keep the process open so that additional feedback can be received from multiple sources across the organization.

Based on the process for data analysis used, feedback usually sorts out according to interrelated themes and issues. I define *themes* as descriptive topics that recur throughout the data that can add meaning to a particular anecdote or comment. For example, in one assessment, professional women reported that their male counterparts always received the "more visible" assignments. The themes that corresponded to this example were favoritism and gender bias. In another setting, sales personnel voiced concern about the need to "relocate" to climb the corporate ladder. The themes associated were organizational bureaucracy and "conservatism."

POSITIVE THEMES

Through the sorting task, strengths as well as limitations of the organization as it relates to diversity can be identified. It is very important to separate out the positive themes and related comments. I always encourage internal personnel to reference these perceived affirmative points and strengths to build a balanced plan of action.

The positive themes are typically generated with introductory questions such as, "What do you like about working here?" or "What do you like about your job?" Common themes are reputable company or organization, good place to work, sense of family, and opportunities for career development. Other questions may invite feedback that elicits enabling characteristics or behaviors. These data can also support the positive themes.

CATEGORIES FOR SORTING

In my work, I have developed a step of subsuming the numerous issues and themes under three major headings: *organizational culture, interpersonal behavior,* and *systems.* For example, in some settings, concerns may be raised about a focus on class divisions; giving preferential treatment to certain members of the organization; the dominant male-orientation; the inability of employees to admit to mistakes; or the messages of inclusion or exclusion communicated by the artwork, magazines, and so forth in the facility. These five issues may be interpreted to suggest that the organizational culture is perceived as classist, sexist, perfectionist, and exclusionary. Needless to say, these blanket terms communicate a particular image about the environment, one that at face value is not favorable.

Labels, however, do not tell it all. It is essential to examine concerns and issues raised under the other two categories. For this discussion, I continue to refer back to these five original issues to see how they play out for the other domains.

Regarding *interpersonal behavior,* concerns may include behaviors that affect individuals, including management practices that seem to favor men for visible and desirable assignments and promotions, work and family flexibility for professional personnel but not clerical staff, lack of developmental opportunities for individuals who are not on management tracks, and disrespectful behavior toward employees manifested through homophobic jokes. The common denominator among these examples is that they represent practices that can have an adverse impact on particular individuals or groups. A more optimistic view is that they are behaviors and practices that can be modified through proactive strategies proposed in the plan.

Typically falling under the *systems* category are issues related to policies and practices that affect different constituencies: career planning, performance evaluations, organizational communications for internal and external use, board or trustee representation, and workload. Many of these specific concerns fall under the critical business systems framework discussed in Chapters 1 and 5. Again, through the formulation of behavioral strategies, it is possible to address most of the issues and concerns reported.

The use of this three-domain framework provides a means to sort issues and concerns more precisely; to identify ones of greater importance or pervasiveness, particularly if they are mentioned repeatedly or under more than one domain; and to recognize the interrelationship between workplace concerns. In addition, by examining these concerns with reference to the organizational diversity mission, leaders and planners are likely to gain a more objective perspective about the adverse affect of particular behaviors on performance and productivity.

Reframing Issues Into Goals and Strategies

It should be evident that the sorting task will yield an abundance of data, requiring a reduction process to make it usable. How can 30 to 50 different concerns and issues be operationalized into goal statements? How will organizational leadership recognize the business value of one goal and strategy versus another? Diversity management planners have taken multiple approaches to address these points.

Table 6.1 shows how individual concerns and issues reflect subcategories under the three domains. The categories that most often emerge are career development; diversity education; interpersonal relations including racism, sexism, homophobia, and classism; management practices such as marketing and advertising; community relations; physical environment; glass ceiling; work and family; performance evaluations; and usually, human resources systems and practices and interpersonal and organizational communications; among others. Data from different organizations and industries indicate that these areas manifest both positively and negatively in daily life in a workplace, and consequently benefit some individuals and limit others. In the process of strategic planning, these areas are critical to organizational culture change, and the challenge for diversity committees is to reframe issues and concerns into goals or targets.

Examples. In a health care organization, the proposed domain-specific framework was utilized, yielding more than 60 related issues. Following a sorting process, these 60 issues were collapsed into six goal areas: (a) human resources practices, including recruitment and selec-

TABLE 6.1 Three Domains for Analysis

Organizational Culture Issues/Concerns	Interpersonal Behavior Issues/Concerns	Systems Issues/Concerns
Image Top-heavy, white male management	*Organizational Support Systems* Lack of support systems for new employees, white women, and persons of color in management roles	*Career Advancement* Career paths are not well communicated Information about how to get ahead seems to be based entirely on who you know Glass ceiling in place for persons of color
Preferential Treatment Income-generating departments are more valued and rewarded than those that perform supportive and essential functions	*Disrespectful Workplace Behavior* Disrespectful communication among employees, e.g., telling of ethnic and sexist jokes	*Performance Evaluations* Performance evaluations invite too much subjectivity "Who gives management their evaluations?"
Ambiance Physical appearance of the facility does not communicate a sense of inclusiveness to employees and clients who use the services	*Management Practices* Inconsistent management practices that communicate subjectivity and preferential treatment	

tion; (b) workload balance; (c) interpersonal communication; (d) diversity awareness and education; (e) customer service; and (f) culturally competent medical practices task forces were assigned to clarify the issues for each area and to develop action plans. This provided the needed focus for strategy development.

At a manufacturing firm, six major areas were also identified: (a) work and family, (b) compensation and benefits, (c) performance evaluations, (d) gender bias and sexual harassment, (e) management practices, and (f) career development. Under each area appeared a number of related issues and concerns. The representative committee generated recommendations to support the restated goals.

Following sorting and clarifying processes, a regional bank identified five strategic diversity goals: (a) leadership, (b) education, (c) hiring and promotion practices, (d) marketing, and (e) community service. Rather than create one strategic master plan for all banks and departments to follow, leaders requested plans to support these goals from the appropriate business lines. For example, human resources representatives, the diversity director, and regional diversity committees were charged with developing strategies for education and hiring and promotion practices. A committee of senior-level managers was charged with preparing a leadership-driven diversity plan. The intent was to have more individuals assume responsibility for designing and directing diversity strategies.

A consumer products company used a corporate-based council to establish strategic goals, as many similar issues had emerged across different business units and locations. The goals were communicated to divisions, which in turn established local plans to support them.

There is no limitation to the number of goals and strategies recommended or action steps that can be developed. Ultimately, the design and implementation of a strategic plan requires customization and a system for accountability. Who is responsible for implementation? Is there a time line? What are the consequences if goals are not supported? These additional questions can be built into goal-specific action plans or addressed through other means. Minimally, however, they need to be anticipated and communicated at the time strategic plans are set. An example of the format used in a manufacturing facility is provided. The executive team developed an accountability process for each of their major goal areas:

A Diversity Strategic Action Plan

Goals			
Strategy	Responsibility	Time Line	Measurement of Change

Another Approach for Goal Setting

I continue to emphasize that there is more than one approach that can be followed to translate findings into goals and strategies. The domain-specific framework previously discussed allows for the emergence of goal areas, such as career development, management development, marketing and advertising, diversity education, community relations, communication, and performance evaluations, among others. These topics become unifying categories for discrete issues and concerns that reflect interpersonal behavior, organizational culture, and systems.

For example, under the heading of career development could fall issues of succession planning, career guidance and pathways, mentoring, developmental opportunities, and glass ceiling. Although career development may be considered systems related, glass ceiling usually reflects organizational culture, and developmental opportunities may hinge on interpersonal behavior between management personnel and individuals. Through a reframing process, an overall goal statement regarding career development can be made, followed by a set of enabling strategies to address the multiple concerns.

EXAMPLE

Goal. Our goal through career development is to create programs, policies, and guidelines that will help all sales personnel be successful. Our plan addresses the following areas: mentoring, job opportunities, management practices, and relocation.

Strategies:

- ❑ Develop a formal and voluntary mentoring program for sales personnel.
- ❑ Establish a study group by the end of Year X to explore mentoring examples in other organizations.
- ❑ Each employee should work with management above her or his immediate supervisor at least twice a year.
- ❑ Revise the current relocation policy to assist in the employee's career development opportunities.
- ❑ Establish an annual employee training contract for each person and review on a semiannual basis.
- ❑ Have Human Resources prepare a succession planning report to address glass ceiling concerns.

Work and family is another area that tends to reflect a myriad of concerns and needs of a diverse workforce (see Table 6.2). Among the issues often cited are flexible work schedules, dependent care (for

TABLE 6.2 Work-Family Balance

Concerns	Recommendations
There is a concern over the number of times people are required to relocate over the course of their career.	Communicate current direction of relocation policy.
Lack of time for family as a result of work load and travel.	To further develop the organizational skills of the sales force: • Have semiannual manager visits to reps' home office for reinforcing skills on processing information • Provide training information for time management • Preserve the integrity of weekends/holidays/personal time when scheduling meetings/functions.
Children and/or marriage as a hindrance to promotion, i.e., leaving meetings to pick up children at day care.	Meet with manager to develop a clear understanding of the impact of marriage and/or children on career development. Provide training to managers as it relates to marriage and/or family issues and career advancement.
Lack of child care assistance as it relates to sales reps who are traveling.	Communicate the current child care reimbursement policy provided by the company.
Lack of knowledge about options for sales personnel.	Have the comps and benefits personnel attend at least one national meeting with us to answer questions.

children, elderly parents, or an ill partner or spouse), bereavement leave, and career planning. Through needs assessments, I continue to note that this area still seems to reflect concerns most widely introduced by women. For example, women in professional and managerial assignments often seek input about how their careers will be affected if they take time off for child rearing. Similar questions could be relevant for men who might choose to participate in child rearing or employees who leave full-time work to pursue higher education full-time. Another type of concern is raised by gay and lesbian employees. The policies and procedures regarding dependent leave or bereavement time of many organizations reflect the needs of heterosexual couples and families, leaving the gay and lesbian group behind.

For diversity planners, the goal or target area that obviously emerges is that of work and family policies and practices. In some organizations, committees develop the strategy statements and necessary tasks to address the target area. In others, specific departments or business units develop their own strategies. For this particular issue, input from human resources personnel is essential.

Still another commonly identified action area is organizational communications. Receiving outdated and late information, the perceived withholding of information, or using only written memos to communicate are examples typically raised during data gathering. With organizational communications as a goal area, some organizations value enabling strategies such as consultation from communication experts and establishment of cross-functional task forces to develop action plans. In large organizations with communications departments, the issues may still exist. This may require reexamining the focus of the tasks assumed by the communications department. Is it primarily external? If so, what is the quality of the communication? A number of goals require the use of both internal and external resources.

Community relations has emerged as an increasing area of need when discussing diversity strategies. This has been particularly relevant for human services agencies and cultural institutions designed to serve the public sector. Because their existence depends on the attendance or involvement of people in the local area, the needs and expectations of a changing market require attention. One social services agency I worked with found itself challenged by some community activists who thought too many immigrants were receiving services to the exclusion of longtime residents. Rather than taking a defensive posture, the agency director took proactive strategies. He invited immigrant and nonimmigrant residents to meet together to examine the systems for delivery of services to all people. "Trying to fix or react did not make sense. I thought I was delivering services fairly and evenly but also realized that changing perceptions can be an impossible task," reported the agency executive director. The cross-cultural task force that formed became a visible model in the community and actually promoted a positive external perception of the agency.

In another example, a cultural institution recognized through its attendance surveys that participation by persons of color was extremely low. Close proximity to ethnic and racial minority communities made this fact even more glaring. To address community relations, the staff employed different outreach strategies: convening leaders from community agencies to brainstorm the concerns, partnering with local public schools to bring children from these communities to the institution, creating multicultural exhibits, hosting an open house for individuals from specific ethnic and racial minority groups, and developing marketing materials in languages other than English. This multistrategy approach brought results over time. Attendance increased, and as school children reached working age, they began to seek part-time job opportunities at the institution.

The point of this discussion is to underscore the need to get as "close as possible" to some of the issues. Through careful analysis of the findings, looking at what they say about current practices, and a willingness to try new behavior, goals can be reached.

The Prioritization of Goals and Strategies

Most organization leaders say that all of their diversity goals have equal merit and that it is important to address all of them. In reality, however, limitations and priorities dictate what is pushed forward. These factors may take the form of available resources—human and capital, related business imperatives, timing, and other internal or external forces.

In one company, it was presumed that racism would be the most important barrier to feeling valued and to being promoted in the workplace. Through the assessment, it was learned that issues related to gender bias and sexual harassment were more pronounced. Needless to say, resources were committed to initiate multiple, action-oriented strategies.

The size of the organization may also influence goal prioritization. In small institutions or ones geographically centralized, it is likely that the strategic plan will be implemented uniformly across different settings. In national and multinational companies with large business units, there may be more autonomy, allowing diversity planners discretion about the goals and strategies that are prioritized.

Are These Really Diversity Strategies?

During my presentation of a strategic plan to an executive management team, I was met with quizzical looks and then questions. What does workload have to do with diversity? Is relocation a diversity issue? Although I was prepared to respond to the questions, it was a little surprising to hear them at this stage in the process. As I advised the diversity administrator and her committee, these questions were like a wake-up call reminding all of us that others in the organization might not have a clear understanding about diversity.

When questions such as these arise during a diversity initiative, I encourage the diversity planners to ask the following questions: How has diversity been defined within the organization? Has it been circumscribed to only race and gender? Or is it a matter of perception? It is reasonable to assume that no matter how explicitly the diversity initiative may be described as "involving all personnel," there will still be individuals with selective hearing who prefer to link diversity with affirmative action. Although all persons may not want to accept the scope of the diversity management, it still behooves planners and their consultants to engage in more deliberate planning about how to communicate information about the initiative. Being close to the process, as are most committees, they are likely to generalize their breadth of awareness and knowledge about diversity to the rest of the organization. The vice president for diversity in an insurance firm described the committee as ambassadors. They were carrying messages about the initiative but also getting feedback from peers and managers. These data were a form of reality testing, informing the committee how information was being heard and interpreted. If misunderstandings or complaints were aired, committee members could deal with them immediately and not be taken by surprise at a later point.

Enablers of Strategic Plans

Three key considerations in moving a diversity strategy forward throughout the organization are communication, credibility, and accountability. Without operationalization of these processes, the best of strategies are likely to remain in a document with a limited shelf life.

COMMUNICATION

At this point, planners may want to ask themselves what procedures have been used to transmit information about the process and progress of the diversity initiative? Who have been the messengers? If communication has been minimal or relied on only written communiques, the possibility for confusion is greater. Communication about the organization's strategic diversity goals must flow along the path of previously recommended communication efforts: multidimensional, verbal and nonverbal, and multilingual if appropriate.

Dissemination of the plan can take many forms. It can be part of an annual report about diversity management goals complete with the stated business rationale for each strategy to be applied. Some organizations identify the major goal areas in their corporate annual report. Profiling an initiative at the highest level of an organization, among stockholders, trustees, and executive management, is essential.

Most diversity audits involve a representative workplace sample. Including employees in general in disseminating information about the program as it unfolds will reinforce one of the primary goals of most initiatives: to create a more inclusive, respectful workplace. In most audits, people-related concerns are widely reported; feedback about how the organization plans to address these issues must be communicated. The possible formats include presentations by managers, internal newsletters, signage around the workplace, and brochures.

CREDIBILITY

As previously mentioned, the strategies designed to support a business goal must be implementable and measurable. These two criteria should be referenced as a plan is developed, communicated, and implemented. Failing to write implementable strategies will lead to a lack of credibility for the initiative and create disappointment among different constituencies for the following reasons: (a) through a needs assessment process, expectations are raised. To not address concerns or to position them as only long-term plans might damage the believability of the initiative; and (b) short-term activities signal the organization is serious about the endeavor, reassuring those who are invested and reminding nonsupporters that the program is "for real."

ACCOUNTABILITY

Accountability is a key concern when it comes to diversity plans. Multidimensional implementation of strategies requires evidence that there is follow through. As has been repeatedly stated, demonstration must begin with senior leadership and management. These individuals should be the visible spokespersons, able to substantially respond to inquiries about direction. In reality, however, it is generally the diversity director and department managers on whom the responsibility for implementation falls. As a consequence, the burden of responsibility also lies with them.

I shall use an example to highlight the importance of accountability. A systems concern that is usually addressed in a strategic plan is performance evaluations. Although most performance evaluations are designed to provide objective feedback, there is also considerable room for subjectivity. What allows a manager to assess fairly two different employees? Are performance and productivity and outcome criteria the overriding considerations? Employee concerns about the fairness and objectiveness of performance evaluations are not unusual, but in my assessments, I found more complaints from white women, persons of color, and individuals in frontline, nonmanagement and nonprofessional roles. Their concerns were that managers did not know them as people and were evaluating them based on white, male norms. Styles of work, interpersonal communication, and other workplace behavior that was perceived to be different by managers counted against these employees. Questions about the instrument used for evaluation were raised, but it was not seen as the major factor to lower ratings. Uniformly, employees stated that they felt their managers related to them primarily based on their visible difference. This led to an awkwardness in communication as well as a degree of self-consciousness for employees, because they perceived that they were not understood and often were treated in patronizing and condescending ways.

Strategies regarding employee evaluations might set forth objectives about reducing bias—a direct response to employee concerns. How might this happen? Employee feedback cites a lack of understanding and sensitivity on the part of managers. Education and training, discussion groups between managers and between managers and employees, and identifying other formats for evaluation might be creative ways to bridge interpersonal and intercultural differences that impact the fair application of performance standards. Ultimately, accountability for this concern and responsive actions must revert to organizational leaders or power brokers. Approving of strategies to address concerns is their responsibility, and from what I have seen in most work settings, employees watch very closely for responses.

Summary

The development and communication of a strategic plan is a serious and time-consuming endeavor. I have described various processes and tasks for taking what may seem to be volumes of data and formulating them into a cohesive and pragmatic road map for action. Sorting, reframing, goal setting, and strategy identification are among the tasks that can contribute to the clear and logical thinking needed by diversity directors and committees. As indicated, the methods taken by a particular organization will be influenced by timing and the nature of the findings themselves. Ultimately, customization allows for the most relevant process for strategic planning.

In my collaboration with organizations regarding the design of a strategic plan, I underscore the fact that my participation in the needs assessment phase enables me to make sense of the data. Responsibility lies with company personnel, but consultants can be excellent facilitators in the process.

Guidelines for Writing the Diversity Strategic Plan

PROCEDURAL CONSIDERATIONS

1. Utilize existing data: vision statement, the business motivators, findings and recommendations from the needs assessment, and available research or learning regarding implementation from other organizations.

2. Establish a work group or committee representative of key constituencies and fully empower it to carry out the task. Define criteria for participation.

3. Communicate priority areas to business units so that they may develop their own action plans as well.

4. Set a time line to guide the process and to ensure continuity and timeliness.

5. Build in a communication process so that the plan can be communicated, beginning with senior management and then carried forward by middle management throughout all levels and business units.

BUSINESS CONSIDERATIONS

6. Base the plan on business goals and measurable outcomes.

7. Establish goals and strategies for the short and long term.

8. Design specific strategies that are implementable and measurable.

9. Expect management override—not everything will be perceived as a business necessity.

10. Expect that not all recommendations will be readily implemented.

11. Include items that require different financial expenditures and identify existing resources that can be dedicated to the implementation of specific strategies.

12. Link strategies to business units and departments to create an integrative approach.

13. Identify sources of accountability.

14. Revisit action plans once strategies have been implemented to ensure their effectiveness.

7

Implementing
Diversity-Related Strategies

❑ How should the implementation of the process be organized?
❑ Who needs to do the work?
❑ What is the role of leadership in the implementation process?
❑ How should responsibility for implementation be assigned?
❑ What are typical reactions to implementation?

❑ My blueprint suggests a natural flow from issue identification to strategic planning. Once a diversity initiative is at the stage where goals and strategies have been identified and presented, the focus shifts to the important task of deciding who will implement them and how implementation will occur. This is a phase where accountability, costs, timing, and scheduling require attention to ensure a cohesive implementation process. During this phase, planners can anticipate varying challenges, forms of resistance, and turf battles, for the changes introduced through diversity-driven strategies will create dissonance for individuals (Festinger, 1957) and the organization.

Employees who do not view the initiative positively might protest about new expectations and responsibilities. Senior-level personnel may argue about implementation costs they have to absorb into their budgets. If a diversity director reports to the chief executive, his or her autonomy from other departments at the time of implementation may be perceived as encroachment, depending on the type of strategy being applied. If an initiative is receiving positive attention, managers may covet responsibility for specific actions for their departments. Very interesting dynamics manifest when implementation begins.

EXAMPLE

Some human resources personnel balked because they did not have a leadership role in the development of the strategic plan. They felt slighted at having a lesser role. Ultimately, a number of implementation tasks fell within their realm of responsibility, allowing some to feel a new sense of control, but others resented the additional assignment.

Who Will Implement the Strategy?

Organizations I have contacted have provided me with many examples of how to approach implementation, and through my discussions, it is clear that there are many successful options and possibilities. It is also apparent that individuals or groups chosen to carry out the specific tasks involved have an important responsibility that requires thorough knowledge about the domain of diversity management and a need for interdependence with other organizational resources. After all, the strategies to be implemented reflect the broad domains of organizational culture, interpersonal behavior, and systems.

As for the question of who will address all or specific diversity strategies, the options are (a) task forces, committees, or councils; (b) departments, business units, or specific constituencies such as occupational groups, boards, trustees, community councils, or consumer or client groups; (c) the office of the designated diversity director and her or his staff; and (d) the most-senior level of the organization, that is, an executive or senior management group that works directly with leadership. Following are some examples.

TASK FORCES, COMMITTEES, OR COUNCILS

This option can take a number of different forms. Task forces, committees, or councils can be designed to include cross-functional, cross-level representation, including seniority and business markets, and individuals representing the other three options proposed here. In some settings, this group with demographic diversity may assume more of a directive and watchdog role—that is, it may accept overall responsibility and leadership for the implementation of an initiative without necessarily being on the front lines in all aspects of implementation. When questions of accountability emerge, it would be this group, however, that would set expectations and manage the process.

In other organizations, these committees or councils become more action oriented, directing and delegating responsibility and even taking on a particular recommendation. For example, in one financial services firm, a committee comprising human resources and training personnel was assigned the task of managing the diversity education strategy. This required the identification and selection of external trainers for their company-specific program. A cultural institution had a diversity committee that included volunteers, staff, administrators, and board members. By working together, they were able to model an interdependent approach to the issues that impacted the organization. Among their goals was the improvement of community relations, a goal the committee itself decided to address. Committee members chose to engage in outreach activities in the neighboring ethnically and racially diverse constituencies, considered potential visitors and members. One of their strategies was to invite spokespersons from the neighborhoods to meet with them. Through these discussions, they were able to overcome existing barriers and identify common areas of interest. Eventually, the committee was able to design organizational activities that were relevant and practical for these communities.

In some instances, the task forces or councils are more homogeneous, comprising primarily management personnel, human resources employees, or white women and persons of color. This last group is particularly contra-indicated in an organization that is not exclusively populated by white women and persons of color. Unless a group of this makeup is directly reporting to leadership, it may be perceived as only window dressing. Homogeneous groups that represent a power base of real authority can be effective because of their ability to drive the implementation process. In a consumer goods company, for example, an advisory council of senior and executive-level administrators provided diversity initiative leadership. Though not implementers, they were perceived to hold the authority to move ahead on the recommended strategic plan.

There are several risks to this approach, however. If council members are perceived as only catering to their self-interests or the interests of special groups, their credibility and that of the entire initiative can suffer. Another possible detriment to this approach is the lack of demonstrated power sharing. The message of "we know best" may be communicated, perhaps creating mistrust or cynicism among employees.

Another risk emerges if the task force members charged with implementation of tasks and interventions are not committed to or knowledgeable about the domain of diversity management or are influenced by internal organizational politics. As a consultant, I have been involved in discussions with internal personnel that suggested "attitudes" on their part. These individuals asked for my input but also wanted me to agree with their way of carrying out specific tasks. In instances like these, I have seen implementation plans flounder, unnecessarily undermining the quality and direction of an organization's plan. Sadly, if those charged with managing the change process are themselves lacking in commitment and ability to implement the initiative's goals, inflexible about sharing power, playing out personal politics, or interested only in self-gain, strategies designed to respond to identified organizational concerns might remain unimplemented.

Although the homogeneous model may seem more efficient because it involves more like-minded individuals, it is important to keep in mind the goals of an initiative. If this group is neither inclusive nor participatory, its makeup might be deemed contradictory.

DEPARTMENTS; BUSINESS UNITS; OCCUPATIONAL GROUPS; OR SPECIFIC CONSTITUENCIES SUCH AS BOARDS, TRUSTEES, COMMUNITY COUNCILS, OR CONSUMER OR CLIENT GROUPS

Another option involves dispersing responsibility for a diversity initiative throughout the organization. This sends the message of shared responsibility and broadcasts that diversity concerns and recommendations lie with all constituencies. In one bank, diversity leadership teams were established for each business unit. The teams were headed by senior executives who in turn reported to their vice president who in turn was accountable to a central advisory committee. The teams were charged with addressing all of the recommendations identified and developing action plans relevant to their particular business units. Action-oriented recommendations were generated by the diversity committee, but there was a realization that each business unit required its own action plan. Through this local-level approach, a sense of ownership was created, a broader and more inclusionary system was put in place, and ultimately the message that diversity relates to business goals of all units became more concrete. According to one bank executive, "Peer pressure drives the work as well. There are more conversations within business lines about what has to be done. Clearly no one wants to fall short."

Another banking leader reported that her team of 10 senior managers was empowered to develop and plan her diversity strategies. "This gives them an opportunity to think creatively and to plan new and innovative activities. If I take on too much of the direct responsibility, which would be easy for me to do, they will lose out. I remember one situation where I previously worked. When I left, the entire special program ended because no one else knew how to direct it. With 10 others besides myself 'in the know,' it is a win-win situation for everyone." In this particular institution, bonuses for executives were also connected to the accountability process. "It's serious work," she said.

Another example comes from an international consumer products company. Leaders decided to charge the human resources directors of their different departments with the leadership responsibility. Their role was to form an ad hoc committee to plan the implementation of the organizational recommendations within the departments. This route gave individuals the autonomy to approach the tasks in their own way while remaining accountable to the steering committee, which included the president, his executive team, and the vice president for human resources. The human resources directors, persons normally charged with addressing people-related concerns and policies, were deemed to have built-in expertise that could contribute to the process. "They know the laws, policies, and procedures, and probably have more contact with employees formally and informally than any other department. It made sense for our group to play a central role," reported the vice president for human resources.

Several executives of human services agencies realized that tacit approval from their board would not make board members more knowledgeable about the real issues facing clients and personnel. Therefore, a diversity committee comprising board members, clients, and employees was established. In another setting, a board created its own diversity committee, allowing it to address many of the same concerns that its agency was addressing, that is, recruiting and retaining board members, marketing in new and creative forums, and reassessing funding sources based on existing agency programs. Through this experiential plan, this board came to recognize the systemic impact of diversity on agency performance and productivity.

BY CONSTITUENCY—AN OCCUPATIONAL GROUP

To assign by constituency means identifying target groups within an organization such as employees, management personnel, customers, boards, and volunteers to carry out the work. This model acknowledges that there are concerns that must be addressed by one or more of the above constituencies. For example, one social services agency decided that its board needed its own diversity action plan, independent of the rest of the organization. It was determined that without the board's leadership, beginning with working on itself, the agency director would not get the buy-in necessary to address the hard issues on a broader scale.

A hospital I worked with decided to target its doctors to carry out diversity tasks. As they are implicit power brokers within the system, the doctors' understanding of the hospital's approach to diversity issues was key. Their daily interactions with patients from low-income communities and culturally diverse backgrounds placed them in a pivotal position, and their ability to help and not alienate patients as well as nurses were deemed business matters. To this end, they were brought in as active strategists to plan and implement relevant recommendations. For example, in this environment male patients were reluctant to be examined by female physicians and nurses. It was determined that education about culture-specific, non-Western medical practices; the dynamics of gender differences in patient-physician; cross-cultural relationships; and the role of power and authority in help giving would assist all physicians in understanding patients' worldviews. A small group also agreed to meet with nurses to examine ways to make their working relationships more respectful and efficient.

In a large, urban setting, a public school system targeted counselors who worked with bilingual students to be part of a 3-year developmental strategy. Self-selected counselors had access to quarterly, half-day trainings to enhance cultural competence. Because these individuals were perceived as change agents, the assumption was that their professional development would have a direct impact on the students with whom they worked.

THE OFFICE OF THE DESIGNATED DIVERSITY LEADER AND HER OR HIS STAFF

One strategy is to empower the designated diversity leader with leadership for overseeing the implementation process. Through this visible assignment, a message about executive-level commitment may be inferred. If the designated leader reports directly to the top or close to the top, the inherent power of the role may be more valued. The challenges for such individuals are many. It is likely that they have already been tested by their peers and other members of the organization. Getting to the stage of implementing strategies suggests that these individuals have already achieved a number of milestones in the process. As was discussed in Chapter 2, the appointment of a diversity director draws considerable attention. With these challenges under his or her belt by this point, credibility is intact and real authority can be exercised.

In a local electronics business, for example, the diversity manager collaborated on an ongoing basis with an advisory council. Together, they held the authority to give direction to, approve, and delegate the implementation of strategies. In an international manufacturing firm, the diversity director asked the company president to name people to an executive advisory council. Those assigned represented some of the highest-level executives in the firm, individuals already empowered as leaders. "Their presence catalyzed and gave visibility to the initiative. Because of who they are, they can influence the actions of resisters. This is very important in an organization where individualism and autonomy are valued," the diversity director said.

A health care organization recognized that addressing the needs of the changing patient base was not going to occur without a deliberate strategic plan and a point person designated to manage the process. In the early stages of the organization's initiative, a vice president was appointed, elevating the initiative to a level of high visibility and responsibility. Through the cultural audit, a number of action areas were identified. The vice president, working with a committee of representatives from different health units, devised a corporate strategic plan and then directed each unit to develop its own. This local approach seemed by far the most favored and acceptable. It enabled the CEO and the diversity vice president to set expectations of senior medical and administrative staff throughout the regionally dispersed organization. "When highly skilled and experienced people are given the freedom to create their own plan of action, they make a statement about what they believe, are committed to, and willing to follow through on. It is a very powerful process," she said.

THE MOST SENIOR LEVEL OF THE ORGANIZATION

Another option is to put responsibility for diversity management in the office of the executive. Although this may be perceived as a statement of power and action, there is still a need to delegate to specific individuals (diversity director) or a department (usually human resources). In one educational institution, the president designated a trustee to lead the diversity charge. Though an outsider to faculty and students, the individual commanded respect and power because of his status as a trustee. Supporting the trustee was a committee constituted of the directors of communications, human resources, and admissions, as well as faculty representatives. Though not the norm, this was a creative approach by the president to give the initiative a level of visibility and legitimacy.

A major cultural institution in Boston took a similar approach. In this case, a member of the board of overseers assumed the initiative leadership, with the expectation that because of her status, she could direct the strategic plan throughout the organization. As a board representative, she was able to communicate with staff as well as clients with greater authority and vision. Manipulative as it may sound, appeals and directives from the organization's highest level of leadership are often the most persuasive. It behooves organizational leaders, nevertheless, to require and expect feedback regarding implementation strategies. They need to know that their managers are giving the initiative the effectiveness they desire. Organization spokespersons indicate that written and verbal reports of progress are generally required.

COMMON DENOMINATORS

This discussion has addressed *how* leadership through a designated person or persons can be leveraged to implement a strategic plan. The four options reviewed often occur together—a committee may exist and oversee the process of business units developing their individual plans. Although there was a designated diversity director in only 50% of the organizations I have worked with, there was still a point person, usually from human resources, with designated duties who relied on the support and authority of the committee. The underlying message is that although there must be a clear and visible presence that moves the process forward, responsibility and accountability for achieving the goals of the plan must be shared broadly.

Simultaneous Strategy Implementation

One bank invited five of its external, customer-focused units to develop their own diversity plans. Simultaneously, the bank began a diversity management training program, introducing it to executive management first. A health care organization began its corporate-centered initiative one year after one of its centers began its process. Once a corporate strategy was developed and announced, other health centers stepped forward. The timing across the centers varied, as did their approaches. This allowed for customized plans, schedules, and resource allocation in the pursuit of the larger organizational goals.

A foundation for the advertising industry identified four major strategies to support its mission. Planners staggered the implementation of the strategies but eventually all occurred simultaneously. These examples indicate that there is no one formula for strategy implementation. Planners in most organizations refer back to motivators for the initiative, issues identified through the needs assessment, and other information they have gathered along the way to determine what goals to prioritize and when to begin.

It should be underscored that because communication is often identified as a goal to support the diversity initiative, it will be enacted simultaneously through different media to support specific strategies.

Mixed Reactions

The implementation of diversity-derived strategies continues to bring both positive and negative reactions in organizations. Individuals who recognize that diversity is about *all people* and performance more quickly see the connection between diversity and the issues addressed. There may be new levels of support and interest as more individuals become involved with task forces, educational programs, or other strategies to address workplace concerns and goals. On the negative side may be the voices of those who believe too much attention is being paid to diversity. These people view the plan only abstractly or even with disdain because they fail to understand the relevance of the initiative to themselves. I have found that trying to convince people of an initiative's benefits is usually not helpful. I have been more successful by simply letting them eventually experience the personal benefits of diversity strategies.

Negative reactions may also come from individuals with high expectations and little patience. These coworkers may want to see results more quickly than is possible and will become critics if the process moves too slowly. Critics need to be taken seriously. Their discontent can seriously damage the progress of a diversity plan. Involving critics in strategy planning and implementation may serve to reduce their complaints about the perceived lack of progress.

Reactions of discontent may also emerge among middle managers, most often ending up with add-on responsibilities because of the diversity plan. Because the motto in many contemporary organizations is to do more with less, these individuals are likely to feel more pressure as well as personal and interpersonal struggles. A manager's personal understanding and feelings about diversity can be a facilitator or barrier in the process. I have witnessed adverse reactions in several environments. One organization included middle managers with minimal diversity education in the selection of vendors. The managers became very focused on the costs and benefits of the initiatives, an area in which they had no real skill or knowledge. Another review team involved middle managers who took a confusing approach in their selection of trainers. Individuals used their own subjective perspectives to challenge potential trainers, representing a less than unified and informed voice. With both examples, the middle managers had responsibility for the diversity initiative added to their work schedule. Although as an outsider I could appreciate the stress and conflict these individuals might experience, I also wondered about their capacity to provide proactive direction to the strategic plan.

It is advisable for leadership to know and be clear about expectations of middle managers and other empowered agents on behalf of an initiative. The role these individuals play can impede or facilitate the process.

Summary

Implementation must be viewed as a short- and long-term process. With many new areas and foci for change, careful planning for delivery of specific strategies must be made. In addition, I have indicated that there are numerous parties and individuals who must be part of the process. It is through their combined leadership and participation that the diversity initiative can continue to gain strength and credibility. The essential point throughout the implementation process is that all members of the organization stand to gain, and this must come across in word and actions.

Guidelines for Implementing Diversity-Related Strategies

1. Carefully plan the implementation process.
2. Recognize the different constituencies who can be part of implementation.
3. Take into account other organizational business when announcing and scheduling plans.
4. Engage leadership to model and set accountability standards.
5. Drive strategies through business units and divisions.
6. Track action and progress through designated business unit heads and a diversity committee.
7. Enable simultaneous implementation of strategies where feasible.
8. Make resource considerations: people, space, time, and money.
9. Recognize the skill, commitment, and willingness of individuals to implement planned strategies.
10. Collaborate with consultants.

8

The Role of Education and Training

❏ What can be accomplished with training?
❏ How can learning be sustained or reinforced?
❏ How can the impact of training be assessed?
❏ Should training be mandatory?
❏ What criteria can be used to select trainers?

❏ According to Tom Peters (1987) in *Thriving on Chaos*, to achieve a sense of empowerment, employees must go through training and retraining. He cites education as the vehicle for transmitting vision and values, and in my experience, well-designed and relevant diversity-related education is a major asset to an organization's master plan for change through diversity.

Education and training have often been considered the essence of a diversity initiative. In some organizations, they are viewed as key to changing attitudes and behavior; others view them as a way to build awareness about valuing differences. When the data from *Workforce 2000* (Johnston & Packer, 1987) first reached many organizations, it provided the impetus for many leaders to use training as the program to define an entire initiative. Over time, many have learned that this single-dimension approach is rarely sufficient to address organizational structures and systems that impact diversity. Although education and training are central to a diversity initiative, it is important to remember that they cannot stand alone. Rather, they make up one strategy among others to support the goals of an initiative. Using this approach, educational interventions are introduced at specific junctures and are often driven by the needs of a particular business unit or department. For example, a bank provides training first for the mortgage and lending department because of the high level of people interaction. Other organizations have begun with human resources personnel. Because their functions are people and policy focused, it is assumed that competency in the area of diversity management is primary.

The purpose of this chapter is to discuss several considerations that can guide choices about the components of an education and training strategy (see Figure 8.1). Nevertheless, organizational planners are encouraged to frame their approach through customized models that will best meet the needs of their diverse, yet industry-specific audiences.

Training Considerations

Before I begin, let me outline several consideration. All of these will be elaborated on as we move through the chapter.

1. Training is but *one* strategy in a diversity initiative. Stand-alone education and training programs without other concurrent strategies to address organizational culture and systems change will have a low impact.
2. Education and training may serve distinct purposes.
3. Training and education programs must be designed in the context of the particular workplace. The methodology used in one setting may be counterculture (and counterproductive) in another.
4. Training must be designed to address behavioral change with specific attention to workplace goals. A focus on attitude change requires a long-term process not easily achieved through time-limited education.

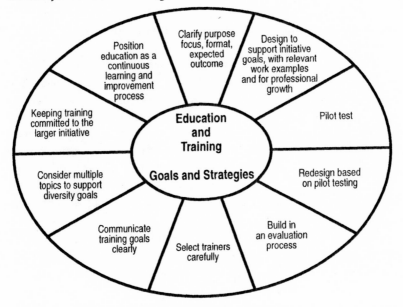

Figure 8.1. Education and Training Goals and Strategies
© Empowerment Workshops, Inc.

5. There are different topics and issues that fall under the purview of diversity, education, and training. How an individual organization defines diversity influences the type of training that is introduced in that setting.

6. Off-the-shelf training should be used with caution.

7. Expertise in cross-cultural issues, diversity management as distinguished from affirmative action, facilitation, teaching, and training design are some of the criteria to look for in a facilitator and instructor. Diversity management is based on research and tried practices that require expertise for implementation. (This is further addressed in the discussion about trainers.)

All of the above considerations are elaborated in the next few sections. They are introduced here to begin to create a mind-set about the complexity and seriousness that surround education and training as a strategy.

Differentiating Between Education and Training

The field of education and training in the domain of diversity management has expanded over the past 10 to 15 years, leading to a growing menu of programs, topics, and videos and other forms of media to address diversity issues in the workplace. In the early 1980s, the Digital Corporation opened a path with its Valuing Differences awareness-building program. In the 1990s, there has been an increased emphasis on skill building and integrated management training programs. This growth makes the planning and decision making about the kind of training and the expected impact on business goals more complex.

Diversity leaders and consultants hold different views about the definition of education and training in the area of diversity management. For some, education is seen as promoting awareness, whereas training, many suggest, addresses awareness as well as knowledge and skills. In fact, the emphasis is on skills. What are skills? According to *Webster's Dictionary* (1977), skills are about expertness, practical ability and knowledge. In many of my conversations with organization spokespersons, skills have been equated with behavior change and the development of new management practices. In some business environments, competency has become a buzzword to describe the standards for measuring performance.

One multinational oil company introduced competency-related language into managers' performance evaluations. Human resources managers were at a loss about assessing competence because they had not defined it or anchored the concept in specific observable criteria.

A hospital administrator indicated that diversity had been designated as a core competency for the organization. Her question was, how do we operationalize this?

A museum included diversity as a criterion on all employees' performance evaluations. The expectation was that through individualized work plans, employees would be able to plan a process that would later allow them to demonstrate competence in diversity.

Again, if we review the definition of competence, it suggests being "properly qualified," "skillful," or "capable" (*Webster's Dictionary*, 1977). To become competent in the domain of diversity and diversity management would logically require competency-based training.

Competency-based training is knowledge based and behavioral in nature, empowering individuals to exercise behavior that supports the goals of a diversity program at two levels: interpersonally and through good management practices. This is a new focus within the realm of diversity education, and it will take shape over time through the criteria specified in this chapter and through lessons acquired in ongoing diversity management education and training across the country.

Some of the resources diversity planners can turn to for models of multicultural, competency-based training come from the fields of counseling, psychology, and health care (Arredondo et al., 1995; Sue et al., 1992). These competencies address the domains of awareness, knowledge, and skills, specifying content and experiential strategies to become competent. These are readily transferrable to business environments because of their focus on interpersonal relationships, for example, with coworkers and from supervisory levels.

Clarity about the meaning of terms that will be used regularly during a diversity education strategy is important to the communication process. Other factors regarding language use include organizational culture and its historical approach to education and training, the intended audience, and the relationship of education and training to other educational programs specific to the diversity initiative and other business goals.

Designing Education and Training Programs

The education and training component of a diversity initiative requires a process that includes planning and design, pilot testing, redesigning, implementation, evaluation, and revision. In the planning phase, a number of questions should be addressed:

- ❑ What are the goals or purposes for the program?
- ❑ Who is the audience?
- ❑ What are the expected outcomes?
- ❑ How will the program be delivered, who will deliver it, when will it be delivered?
- ❑ Will it be customized, off the shelf, or a combination of both?

❏ What types of activities will work best in the existing organizational culture?

❏ How will the education and training be linked to other diversity-driven strategies?

❏ How will the education and training be linked to the organization's or the business unit's goals?

❏ How will the message about training be communicated?

Although each of these questions can be responded to independently, it is also obvious that they are interrelated. Decisions about content naturally depend on the organizational philosophy and intended audience, whereas a communication strategy that supports diversity education is essential for all audiences.

OPTIONS

It is important to view education and training as providing multiple options. Within the realm of building cultural or diversity awareness, there are many variations: Education and training could focus on sexual harassment, gender bias, gay and lesbian concerns, cross-cultural interactions, or cultural awareness. Education and training could also fall under the rubric of diversity management training, human resource-specific orientation to diversity issues, customer service skills from a diversity perspective, and training of marketing and personnel departments to communicate more effectively in a diverse marketplace. The topics that could be addressed are many, and one size does *not* fit all. At this stage in the planning process, it is essential to clarify the nature of the educational program(s) that work best for your workplace and their intended purpose. To introduce a training session or education without paying careful attention to findings and recommendations from a needs assessment or other existing sources of feedback is a mistake. I have often, unfortunately, seen programs that were not well thought out fail miserably.

Another important point to keep in mind as you consider these questions is that diversity-related education and training has to be contextual. It must reflect concerns in a given workplace. Should off-the-shelf training versus customized education or training be employed, care must be given to its relevance. Participants tend to be very savvy and readily question the connection of training to their work life.

The format of a program can vary from executive presentations to multiple-day training programs, retreats, panel discussions, large-group lectures, or train-the-trainer models. Some organizations establish special-interest discussion groups, also referred to as "core groups." These may be organized based on demographic criteria, for example, women managers, black males, or gay employees. As education and training can be interpreted broadly, there are numerous options to bring awareness, knowledge, and skills into an the organization or business.

SETTING GOALS AND OBJECTIVES

In the planning of an education or training program, it should be remembered that goal setting is a priority. Goals offer planners and participants the big picture regarding change through deliberate attention to diversity. Table 8.1 illustrates one way to map out goals, objectives, methodology, and expected outcomes of a program.

Setting the goals, objectives, and expected outcomes of a program provides a road map for its content and methodology. When setting goals and objectives, planners should keep the larger goals of the initiative and specific target areas in mind. For example, if the goal of a diversity education program is to increase cultural awareness to improve workplace effectiveness, the objectives might be (a) to explore personal and historical culture, (b) to identify workplace behaviors that impact relationships, (c) to examine the role of communication from different cultural perspectives, and (d) to identify communication strategies that support workplace effectiveness. These objectives indicate that an *integrated* approach is taken through this training—that is, both cultural awareness and workplace effectiveness are addressed through a focus on relationships and communication.

Good training objectives should always be stated so that they can be responsive to the inquiry, to what end or for what outcome? Thus, if we ask, why are we exploring personal and historical culture? the answers might be, to enable employees to exchange real information rather than relating based on assumptions and stereotypes, and to

TABLE 8.1 Framework for Planning Diversity Education and Training

Training Goal: To manage effectively in a diverse workforce
Target Audience: Senior and middle managers
Group Size: 20
Contact Time: 2 days plus orientation session

Objectives	Methodology	Topics	Expected Outcomes
1. To restate Company X's rationale for diversity management education	Lecture: Review of Company X's business case for diversity	Diversity management not affirmative action	Awareness and knowledge about business cases and impact on performance and business goals
2. To explore personal culture	Small group exercises Simulation; lecture	Motivators	
		Personal culture	Awareness about cultural heritage; self-definition based on social identities; feedback on self-esteem
3. To examine behavioral responses to differences	Video Discussion	Personal and work priorities	
		Self-esteem	
		Self-fulfilling prophecy	Identification of source and formation of bias; recognition of influence of bias on workplace decisions—relationships, hirings, promotions, etc.
		Origins of bias	
		Use of power	
4. To explore communication models		Three steps to cross-cultural flexibility	Perspective taking as it relates to peers, subordinates, and supervisors
5. To plan for action		Management dilemmas	Tools to improve and self-manage interpersonal communication

reduce barriers to interpersonal relationships, thereby leading to improved performance and productivity.

CHOOSING A METHODOLOGY AND FORMAT

The purpose of a program, the audience, time restrictions, and how the program will be applied determine the method and format used for an educational or training program. At one end of the range of formats to choose from are executive presentations, usually involving a lecture format. This format is used primarily with executives, senior-level personnel, and boards. Content is primarily informational, with hard facts and specific examples. The time dedicated to one of these presentations is typically one hour, with additional time provided for questions and answers. An executive presentation on diversity management might include demographic trends nationally and locally (in a given city, state, or region of the country), business approaches to diversity in the same industry or across industries, differentiating between diversity management and affirmative action, the economic rationale for addressing diversity, and a description of my blueprint for successful diversity initiatives. Video clips are often used in an executive presentation.

When deciding on the format for a program, consider whether the subject or participants lend themselves to an interactive or didactic process. As has been discussed above, executive presentations tend to be informational and more didactic. Generally, education and training programs are designed to be more interactive. Possible activities include simulations, role playing, guided imagery, and other experiential exercises. Interactive programs can also include small- and whole-group discussion, written activities, and brief lectures. The media that can be used to supplement or complement a program are wide ranging. These can include readings, films, case studies, video vignettes, and games. Successful educational or training programs usually involve a combination of activities that reflect the culture of the organization and learning approaches typically followed in that environment.

TRAIN-THE-TRAINER FORMAT

Among the different formats to choose from is one called train-the-trainer. This method enables an organization to develop its internal capacity to support change and continue diversity-related work after the departure of external trainers. Train-the-trainer programs also provide developmental opportunities for employees who would otherwise not have reason to teach or facilitate, particularly diversity-related material.

Another factor that supports the use of this method is financial. Many large organizations that want all employees to benefit from an educational or training program view the train-the-trainer approach as more cost-effective. Although there are many reasons to try this format, it carries risks that should be considered. Collaborating with a consultant skilled in this methodology will help ensure quality preparation and implementation by the new facilitators. But it is ambitious to expect that all facilitators will be equally interested and culturally self-aware and comfortable enough to lead a group. As a consultant for this type of program, I have developed guidelines for the selection of facilitators. These guidelines cover three skill areas: interpersonal, technical, and knowledge. In a train-the-trainer program, participants must learn not only the program content but also how to deliver it effectively—not a small challenge. Guidelines are included at the end of the chapter (see Appendix A).

The selection of facilitators for a train-the-trainer format requires careful planning according to skill areas. My process involves several steps: (a) collaborating with internal personnel to establish specific facilitator criteria; (b) announcement of the train-the-trainer program, allowing for nominations or self-nominations; (c) completion of a participant information form by potential facilitators, describing motivation, expectations, and apprehensions; (d) interviews by internal personnel; and (e) availability for the entire training program.

I seek individuals who are credible and respected within the organization, possess leadership qualities, are effective communicators in general, are flexible, and able to relate well to different types of persons.

CONSIDERING THE AUDIENCE

Planning has to take into account the audience of a program. Considerations could include the learning styles of the participants, the mix of the group, literacy levels, participants who speak English as a second language, and relevancy of materials to everyday work life. The feedback I have overwhelmingly received from different businesses who have planned and implemented a program is that the content must be pragmatic—it must connect to daily work experiences to be deemed valuable. The concepts and models used must relate to work situations and issues that require attention. Many participants believe that if they cannot put what they've learned into practice, what is the point?

Another consideration is the level or function of the potential audience. Executive presentations should not be made to support personnel, just as particular simulations and games should not be used with senior executives. Thus, the most successful exercise for one group may insult another. Related to this is the issue of having mixed groups. I am often asked, Is it ok to have people from different levels in the same workshop? The questioners usually mean managers and supervisors. A simple yes or no response is generally not appropriate. Rather, I prefer to raise a set of questions to help planners make their decision. For example, have managers and employees attended training together in the past? What is the nature of the relationship between managers and employees? Autocratic? Interdependent? Is there a reason for having them attend together?

Audience Guidelines. Scoping out the audience usually allows appropriate decisions to be made about format, but I suggest the following guidelines:

1. If it is strictly a didactic presentation, who and how many is not an issue. The main concern should be the length of the presentation.
2. Initial training for supervisory and nonsupervisory personnel should be held independently. If the training design has built-in continuous learning opportunities, then there may be a rationale for having these two levels participate together.
3. Consider an implementation process of contiguous training experiences that is, rather than having all managers attend during the first

year, create a format that will allow the managers of, say, the mortgage department to attend first, followed by the remaining employees in the same department. From a learning standpoint, this arrangement can foster greater mutuality and capacity to focus on similar goals and issues within a circumscribed period of time. Otherwise, training supervisors one year and their supervisees the following creates a gap, limiting the ability of all parties to come together to share and apply their new learning.

What About the Reluctant Participant? Reluctant participants are the nemesis of facilitators, but they need to be expected. For organizational planners, this is also a concern, but one that can be managed through several checkpoints:

1.   The communication strategies employed regarding the training program—how and by whom the message is communicated—are critical factors. When adequate communication has not occurred, participants and trainers are at a disadvantage. The credibility of the diversity initiative and its leaders also comes into question.

2.   Consider the reputation of particular participants. All organizations have their critics and naysayers, and when it comes to diversity, these individuals may become even more vocal. If this can be anticipated, communication on a one-to-one basis with these individuals prior to training by their managers can defuse a potential unpleasant situation and also establish expectations about behavior.

3.   Most trainers involve the participants in the establishment of norms or ground rules before a workshop goes forward. These norms are designed to provide a sense of safety and comfort for all participants.

4.   The skill and credibility of the facilitator is another vital factor. Reluctant participants will challenge both internal and external facilitators—they are usually nondiscriminatory. Nevertheless, individuals must be prepared to address the reluctant participant and keep the training process moving.

TIMING AND SCHEDULING

How much time can be taken for the program without negatively impacting other work responsibilities or people's personal lives? How much education or training can a given audience reasonably participate in and absorb? All participants have saturation points. I know of intensive-training models that involve 12-hour days, evening work, or weekend time. If the purpose of this type of intensive training is clear with respect to its application, it may be more meaningful, but programming that caters to the needs of the trainers and does not sufficiently assess the impact on participants may be misguided. (In a separate section, trainers will be discussed.) I recommend an incremental-training model, with the introduction of a given topic followed by related educational programs over a period of years.

What is the optimal time to schedule training? Are there other competing priorities? The best-laid plans must take timing into account. Some general rules of thumb are never to schedule programs on Monday mornings or Friday afternoons. After-dinner and weekend sessions should also be carefully considered before scheduling. There are also particular times of the year that are less than optimal, for example, national holidays, an organization's vacation periods, or public school vacation time. To not take participants' likely prior commitments into account might frustrate both participants and planners.

PILOT TESTING

All training and education programs can benefit from pilot testing. Ideally, the sample group who tests the program should reflect the ultimate participants. In some settings, pilot testing may occur with representatives from human resources, the diversity committee, or other hand-selected individuals. To ensure the smooth delivery of a program, testing its material, activities, and so on is well advised. I also encourage revisions after a program has been launched. Feedback from participants can help to improve the context and process.

Education and Training as a Process, Not an Event

How education and training are thought of within a business or corporate community influences expectations. For example, if training is the cornerstone of an organization's initiative, it might be thought of (erroneously) as the "answer" to all diversity-related concerns. If the goals of the program are too lofty, planners will likely be disappointed when they do not achieve their goals.

As an educator, I believe diversity education and training programs must be part of a deliberately designed learning process. This incorporation can take different forms:

1. Anchor the program goals in the mission of the diversity initiative itself, demonstrating relevance and context.
2. Provide orientation sessions or a formal presentation for coworkers by a key management representative to lay out the rationale for the program.
3. Integrate actual business concerns and goals into the training.
4. Have participants complete an action plan, specifying their plans to apply the materials taught.
5. Have participants complete a program evaluation, informing trainers and planners of the strengths and limitations of the content, methodology, and so on.
6. Provide follow-up educational opportunities in the form of discussion groups, coaching sessions, additional training, or other media.

Thinking about and positioning diversity-related education and training as part of an ongoing process to promote organizational business goals rather than as an event in and of itself allows both planners and participants to have more realistic expectations for what it will accomplish. When collaborating with organizations, I talk about education as developmental, a process that requires continuity, consistency, relevance, and accuracy. When it comes to diversity education and training, similar standards should apply. With organizational diversity goals and learning criteria directing the design and planning process, diversity education and training is less likely to become a scapegoat if nothing changes organizationally. Demonstrating the practical, day-to-day value that can be gained through education will make it something people look forward to rather than dread.

MANDATORY TRAINING

There are different schools of thought about voluntary versus mandatory diversity training. In my experience, organizational leadership and culture are key factors. Where the leaders model by participating in training efforts and communicating to the entire workforce their expectations about attendance, mandatory training can be more feasible.

Allowing voluntary attendance sends two messages: (a) individuals can determine the importance or nature of the program, and (b) leadership is not supporting the training and the overall initiative. With mandatory training, how the expectation is communicated and by whom become critical to employees' reactions.

Communicating About Education and Training

Diversity-related education and training programs should not be unpleasant or feared by participants. To ensure this, it behooves planners to give careful thought to the communication process surrounding the programs. Most trainers I have spoken with tell war stories about participants who did not want to be involved in a program and who challenged them. This places an unfair burden on the trainer and distracts all participants from the session itself. Although any form of education and training in the workplace should be approached with thorough planning as I have discussed, diversity-related programs require extra sensitivity. There are many ideas associated with diversity—some people equate it with affirmative action, others look forward to it as a new learning opportunity, and some think of it as punitive.

Clear communication about diversity education can help smooth the variety of reactions participants will come with. This involves (a) developing an official statement from the leadership of the organization about the importance of the education and training strategy; (b) preparing management personnel to carry the message about the program's goal; (c) preparing a script for management personnel with commonly asked questions and answers about diversity-related training and education; (d) having the message about programs communicated by employees' direct supervisor or manager; (e) inviting rather than telling future participants about their involvement in the training; and (f) thanking participants for their support of the training through follow-up communication.

The Impact of Education and Training

In addition to setting goals and objectives, planners must also project the expected impact. What will be different as a result of the training? What change can be expected? Most people would agree that training alone cannot transform participant behavior, particularly if plans for change related to critical business systems are not in place. Minimally, however, planners should be able to inquire about areas of impact that will in turn allow for the identification of some measures of progress.

Some organizations establish measures or indicators of change based on training and education programs alone, talking specifically of its costs and benefits. This is a very ambitious way to measure change, considering the limitations that surround time-limited programs. Attempting to assess change should take into account all strategies that relate to the initiative. In other words, a comprehensive evaluation is recommended rather than one that looks only at training and education. (Evaluation of initiatives will be discussed at length in Chapter 9.)

In any event, it is advisable to assess the impact of education and training programs, and this can be done in a cost-effective and efficient manner:

1. Conduct evaluations at the end of the specific program and inquire about what will be most helpful in the workplace.
2. Introduce a follow-up evaluation one month after a program to ask participants what was most useful about the training and how it helped them. (You don't need to ask many questions, just get the highlights about what stayed with participants.)
3. Ask for feedback 3, 6, and 12 months later. Participant returns may drop off, but you will still gather helpful feedback for future planning.

I offer several cautions for creating an evaluation form. Identify areas of "impact" rather than "change," as this may be more acceptable in the context of the program itself. Use the feedback from evaluations to inform later programs. Planners, trainers, and organizational leaders should keep in mind that there are many factors that contribute to learning and how learning is applied. This caution relates to diversity education as well.

The Role of Trainers and Facilitators

Key figures in any diversity program are the trainers or facilitators themselves. Their role as designers and implementers of the organization's program must not be underrated. The use of trainers and facilitators varies; in most settings I am aware of, trainers come from outside the workplace.

How can an organization know what criteria to use for selection? How can I tell if it is the facilitator or the material that is not working? The selection of a trainer or facilitator involves several checkpoints to ensure that he or she is a good match for your business: diversity education competency, technical competence as a facilitator, and interpersonal rapport.

Diversity education competency can be measured by the following minimum standards: philosophy and knowledge about the differences between affirmative action and diversity management; familiarity with *Workforce 2000* (Johnston & Packer, 1987); the use of interdisciplinary training approaches; familiarity with and recognition of the business reasons for diversity; and understanding of the distinction between different types of training—oppression based, prejudice reduction, person centered, competency based, multidisciplinary, and awareness building.

Technical competence can be measured by an individual's capacity to design a training program with specific outcomes, to work collaboratively with internal personnel, to meet deadlines, and to provide evidence from previous clients of excellent performance. Some might argue that a trainer or facilitator's interpersonal rapport should be the first priority, but the comments of experienced organizational spokespersons do not agree with this premise. Although they report wanting a consultant who is friendly, helpful, and flexible, they are aware of the importance of the individual's expert and technical competence. This normally includes both expert (knowledge and experience) and facilitative skills—group dynamics, classroom management, and the flexibility to adjust to participant groups, for example, clerical, managerial, occupational (e.g., engineers, nurses).

The past 5 to 8 years have seen an abundance of consultants who describe themselves as diversity trainers. Through personal observations and feedback from other consultants and organizational personnel, I have developed additional criteria that can help you discern whether the consultant you are considering has the skills required to be called a diversity trainer:

1. A background in organizational behavior, social services, or applied psychology
2. Experience teaching high-school or college-age students and adults in a work setting
3. Membership in professional associations related to diversity, organizational development, cross-cultural issues, and so on.
4. Prior work experiences (before becoming a consultant) in multicultural settings
5. Volunteerism
6. Travel
7. Bilingual capacity
8. Cultural self-awareness
9. Academic or experiential evidence of competence

Authenticity is very important in this field. Consultants can make an organization's initiative gain positive recognition through their performance. Choose carefully.

Who Selects Facilitators and Trainers?

I have outlined guidelines for selection of trainers and facilitators but also believe that qualifications must apply to those who make the decisions. Over the years, I have seen great unevenness in this regard, because some decision makers are not knowledgeable about diversity management or experienced in training and facilitating groups. Those who have training backgrounds may not appreciate the specialized knowledge and experience necessary to do diversity training. I have seen these individuals focus only on technical competence, isolating it from the expert nature of diversity management knowledge. Some decision makers also may not be fully committed to the diversity process. Their ambivalence or lack of commitment can easily contribute to biases, leading to greater subjectivity than objectivity about a trainer's competence.

When organizations establish teams for the purpose of selecting trainers and facilitators, they need to be sure that there is a balance of expertise and that these individuals' belief in the benefits of education and training for diversity management is firm, not ambivalent.

Summary

I have a lot to say about training because I recognize the overattention or centrality it has been given in most diversity initiatives. I believe that education and training are critical strategies to carrying out organizational diversity goals but stress that they must be viewed as part of a comprehensive strategy, not as stand-alone events. My goal was to map out a process to follow with numerous factors to consider along the way. In my experience, attention to these factors during the planning and design phase is more likely lead to successful outcomes and satisfaction for all parties involved.

One additional factor I would like to discuss is that of cost. Over the years, I have been told by diversity planners that training costs too much, that they would like to get the "best" possible for the lowest price, that they made a mistake because they sacrificed quality for cost, or that they paid big bucks and received an unsatisfactory program. This question may sound familiar to planners and consultants alike and will continue to be raised in the future. As a consultant, I encourage planners to be clear about goals and expectations for training. Building skills and competency requires more than a one-day training. If diversity competency is going to become part of a performance evaluation, sufficient education and training must be provided individuals so that they can meet this requirement. Again, this involves several educational interventions and that means more expense.

I emphasize the premise that training is but one factor in an overall change process. To rely exclusively or too heavily on training as the heartbeat of the diversity initiative is erroneous. Rather, I advise diversity planners to step back, review my blueprint, and evaluate the role of training. Make sure you position it to promote and advance the initiative, not hinder it.

Guidelines for Education and Training

1. Develop a plan to guide your process.
2. Position education and training programs as one strategy, not as the whole initiative.
3. Clarify the types of programs to be delivered to specific audiences.
4. Be certain that training and education goals are consistent with the goals of the initiative and recommendations from the needs assessment.
5. Recognize the limitations of the impact of training and education.
6. Include pilot testing in your program plan.
7. Develop strategies to assess the impact of programs over 12 months.
8. Have a sound rationale for using a train-the-trainer approach.
9. Have a detailed communication process throughout.
10. Select trainers and facilitators based on predetermined criteria.
11. Consider education and training as a learning process, not an event.

APPENDIX A

Criteria for Selection of Facilitators for Train-the-Trainer Programs

Demographic Considerations

- ❑ Cross-section of departments, functional groups, and so on
- ❑ Balanced representation of the workforce in terms of gender, race, age, sexual orientation, and so on
- ❑ Range of seniority

Interpersonal Criteria

- ❑ Good reputation
- ❑ Trustworthy
- ❑ Informal, positive leader
- ❑ Reliable
- ❑ Flexible; open to differences and change; open to new learning
- ❑ Open to cross-cultural differences
- ❑ Self-management capacity
- ❑ Demonstrated intercultural relationship interests
- ❑ Nonjudgmental
- ❑ Able to receive positive and critical feedback
- ❑ Able to give positive and critical feedback
- ❑ Cultural self-awareness
- ❑ Willingness to have ideas challenged
- ❑ Able to be a "gray" thinker
- ❑ Able to manage discomfort

Skill Sets or Potential

- ❑ Understands teaching and skills required
- ❑ Group facilitation
- ❑ Communication: active listener, raises questions, asks for clarifications
- ❑ Flexibility
- ❑ Role-taking capacity
- ❑ Analytical
- ❑ Open to problem solving
- ❑ Open to new learning
- ❑ Informal mentor to others
- ❑ Risk taking
- ❑ Knowledge
- ❑ Recent student
- ❑ Previous culture-related workshops, coursework
- ❑ Interpersonal or communications course
- ❑ Cultural self-awareness

9

Evaluating Progress and Change

- ❑ How can progress and change be measured?
- ❑ How can success be defined?
- ❑ When is the best time for an evaluation?
- ❑ What types of change can be anticipated?

Throughout this book, I have underscored the need to provide a business rationale, a sense of logic, and behavioral criteria to diversity management. Employing an approach that includes planning and clarification procedures throughout becomes even more critical at the time of a formal evaluation.

• Three years into an initiative, leaders at a manufacturing firm asked for an evaluation of progress. They had proceeded through various phases in my blueprint and were busy implementing various systems and programmatic strategies. During the strategic planning process, they had also projected potential changes that could

---

Author's Note: This chapter was developed with the help of Dr. Richard Woy.

result from the work. Understandably, they wanted to know, how are we doing?

• The executive committee of an advertising foundation made diversity a priority in the communications and advertising industry. Foundation staff instituted four interrelated programs to support their diversity goals. After 6 years, the committee decided to explore the impact of these programs. Were they achieving the desirable results? What changes were evident?

• A health care organization introduced several systems-related changes in response to recommendations made during a needs assessment. What was the impact? How did employees perceive these changes?

Without clear objectives and plans to assess progress and outcomes at critical times, very valuable data may be lost. It has become quite predictable that when organization leaders lament the continuation of workplace concerns and issues in spite of interventions, an assessment strategy was probably not part of the overall strategic plan. My consultation over the past 10 years with organizations engaged in change-oriented initiatives has provided me with numerous opportunities to assess the progress and impact of different strategies and interventions. Not all of my evaluations were specific to diversity initiatives, but they did hold in common the theme of *change* driven by particular organizational goals.

As with all other phases in my blueprint, the evaluation task requires planning and design. Careful and methodical deliberation enables planners to (a) clarify the purpose and scope of the evaluation, (b) clarify the information sought from the process, (c) determine how the data will be used, and (d) check on timing and logistics. Many organizational leaders, although objectively believing that an evaluation will be valuable, may still wonder what the benefits of an evaluation are.

In this chapter, I outline and discuss the fundamentals of carrying out an evaluation. The information covered includes attention to the purpose and basic assumptions of evaluations, types of evaluations, options for methodology and procedures, and possible outcomes from the process. The ideas presented here are drawn from the many evaluations I have conducted in both for-profit and nonprofit settings. Of particular importance is a multiyear evaluation I assisted with that was focused on diversity initiatives in more than 50 human services and cultural institutions. Through my work, I found that similar principles for evaluation can be applied in corporate settings.

Assessment and *evaluation* are terms that I use interchangeably in the following pages. Both words suggest the goal to find value; to measure quantitatively and qualitatively; and to determine viability, effectiveness, and impact. With respect to diversity management initiatives, evaluation procedures are usually designed to understand (a) attitudinal and behavioral changes in predetermined areas, (b) the impact of specific interventions and strategies to promote change, (c) the integration of particular strategies in business systems and policies and practices (i.e., making diversity an area of competence on performance evaluations and offering mentoring for those who request it), and (d) gains in profitability (i.e., market share, income, and other indices of a return on investment) (see Figure 9.1).

Planning and Design

As has been previously stated, planning and design are key to a useful and efficient evaluation process. Measuring for the sake of measuring or assessing in ways that fail to elicit the necessary, relevant information is a waste of time and resources. As a consultant, I approach this task with the same deliberateness applied to any task in my blueprint. Quite often, I have found myself working with organizational planners for whom evaluation is a new procedure. This means that my most important first step is to provide my clients with enough information to allow them to feel comfortable about evaluations and to be able to discuss the process with others, such as managers or the diversity committee. On many occasions, I have presented this information to entire committees so that all parties, not just the diversity director, will be knowledgeable about the process and procedures involved. As with any new strategy, clarification about purpose, basic assumptions, criteria, and expected outcomes are initial elements in a planning discussion.

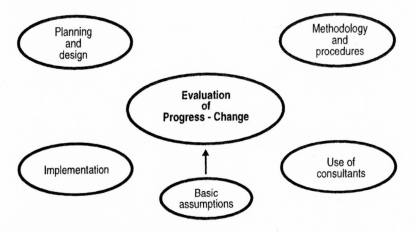

Figure 9.1. Evaluation of Progress or Change

PURPOSE

Why evaluate? Typical reasons for evaluations are to acquire data that point to change or impact based on a planned intervention or program. For example, if a child care program is established on the work premises to reduce the need for parents to leave the workplace, several types of inquiries might be made. Are parents using the facility? Are there fewer disruptions in the areas where the employees work? Has absenteeism, late arrival, or early departure been reduced? How have performance and productivity been impacted?

In the context of diversity initiatives, planners are often motivated by the need to measure a return on the financial and human resources invested. They have indicated to me that they are looking for evidence of impact. I believe that an initiative with clearly articulated goals and objectives deserves to be evaluated. If an organization has spent time and money implementing a number of diversity strategies, it is only logical to examine what has changed, which strategies are working and which are not, and what can be learned from the process thus far. An example comes from organizations that set recruitment, hiring, and selection of underrepresented individuals as a target goal. Their strategies may include outreach in local communities for entry-level personnel, on black college campuses for professional staff, or through culture-specific headhunter agencies for more senior level positions.

Very simply, are these strategies enabling the attainment of the established goal? If yes, a follow-up question often is, What are retention rates?

Evaluations can also help an organization (a) identify enablers and barriers to overall success, (b) provide feedback about how to make strategies more effective, (c) inform planners of how different constituencies are responding to and participating in change-oriented endeavors designed to have a positive impact on personal empowerment and performance, and (d) discover possibilities for replication of the work being carried out by the initiative. Through evaluations, indicators of *permanent* change relative to the stated goals can be identified, be they the behavior of management personnel, modifications or changes in the organization's business systems and management practices, or the ambiance of the institution. By including an evaluation early on, planners can be better prepared to clarify or redefine existing objectives, priorities, strategies, and time lines. Finally, an evaluation can bring the process full circle. It can reaffirm that a diversity management approach has facilitated and can continue to facilitate the types of changes that are congruent with the organization's business rationale; mission and values; competitive position in the industry; and interpersonal stability with regard to employees, vendors, customers, and the community in which it resides.

Basic Assumptions

Everything I have outlined thus far about a diversity management initiative based on my blueprint suggests the need for a knowledge-based understanding of each process or action that is undertaken. The evaluation process is no different. Is it perceived fearfully? Some may greet the announcement of an evaluation with the certainty that the organization will only get bad news. Others may think that assessments will take too much time. Those who resist the process are likely to hope for bad news. If there have been previous negative experiences conducting evaluations, resistance may also manifest.

Again, organizational planners and leaders must become visible and communicate the rationale and potential benefits of the evaluation. They must speak from a mind-set that inspires confidence and optimism about the process, framing the experience as a learning opportunity. In preparing an evaluation plan, organizations need to keep in mind these basic premises:

❑ Evaluations are tools for learning and discovery. Through feedback gathered in the process, it is feasible to understand what is working and what may not be proceeding as expected. Indices of progress, directions, or trends can be identified that are based on deliberately set objectives. Evaluations can reveal indicators of cultural change and the institutionalization of specific practices.

❑ Diversity strategies are interventions designed to promote change; in the evaluation process the impact and effects of specific interventions can be determined.

❑ Evaluations need to be viewed as interventions. Carrying out an evaluation introduces procedures designed to help individuals inquire and learn. Through discussions and surveys, many constituencies have the opportunity to address questions about the initiative. This experience may lead to both positive and negative feedback, new learning (through hearing others' comments), and further relationship building and mutual understanding between participants.

❑ Feedback from evaluations enables management to adjust or modify the strategic plan. Because initiatives are designed to promote change, discovering just what changes occur can reinforce or reclarify the objectives and the ongoing activities. For example, if different business units charged with implementing diversity plans are not meeting this goal, an ongoing evaluation would help to determine the reasons for this. With reliable data in hand, alternative approaches can be attempted.

❑ Evaluations highlight the relationship between employees and management, reducing skepticism. They send a message that management wants to know employees' opinions and demonstrate that the diversity initiative is more than just another good idea or the latest business trend. By conducting a self-study, the message management sends is: There is nothing to hide—we want to know and learn.

❑ Evaluations typically generate "unexpected" findings. These can have several effects. The unexpected may be the discovery of desirable change that had not been projected by the initiative. For example, interaction between employees *across* departments may improve when interaction *within* departments is promoted. This type of side effect is always welcome. Conversely, receiving negative feedback or discovering no change could also be unexpected.

❑ Assume that there will be negative reactions and problematic feedback. In the arena of diversity management initiatives, backlash is not unusual.

It may come from individuals who feel left out, resist the plan for a range of reasons, or believe something different should occur. Sometimes the "best" supporters can also be the worst critics.

Criteria

An evaluation should be relevant to initiative goals and objectives. In Chapters 6 and 7, the discussion of designing and implementing diversity strategies emphasizes the need to set measurable objectives. During the evaluation, the organization can learn if specific strategies are being actualized and to what extent. Simply stated, evaluations must be designed to inquire about, assess, and in as many ways as possible address targeted goals and expected outcomes. For example, if one of the objectives is to increase workforce interaction by building cross-functional teams or developing cross-level diversity committees, there must be specific measures to determine this. How many cross-functional teams have been established? How many cross-level committees have been established? How do participants on these teams and committees experience the interactions? What other factors are contributing to the goal of increased interaction?

Evaluations should inquire at both macro and micro levels. All evaluations must be grounded in major questions or areas of inquiry. What type of impact has occurred? What are barriers or problems in the process? What are enablers to the initiative objectives? What are highlights, successes, disappointments? This level of inquiry can provide more comprehensive data and a broader view about change and impact.

Through the use of specific or more-discrete questions, inquiries about particular objectives and strategies that support initiative goals can be made. For example, if one objective was to increase a diverse representation among management personnel, a specific question could determine the status of this objective: change or no change and how much. If there is an objective to eliminate sexist joking in the workplace, discrete questions could be used to measure the success or failure of this objective and also identify factors that contributed to this result.

Evaluations should measure and identify indices of change and integration of new practices that benefit a diverse workforce. One of the earlier steps in the strategic planning process was to state *expected outcomes*. Related to the goals and objectives of an initiative, statements of expected outcomes typically describe projected behavioral changes at individual and organizational levels. Accordingly, measures and indices of change can be set. These measures can be both qualitative and quantitative, allowing for different examples of change. I could use the example from the previous paragraph, phrasing it as an expected outcome: As a result of the various group-focused interventions, there will be an increased sense of being valued among all employees. Through a quantitative approach, incidents and anecdotes can be tabulated and compared to baseline data. Applying qualitative methods, employees can be asked to describe how they feel about their interactions with peers and supervisors, and how they think this affects their performance.

The most compelling examples of permanent or institutional change are found with the development or refinement of policies and procedures. As was discussed in the earlier chapters, many issues and concerns related to organizational systems are identified as factors that exclude or otherwise adversely impact different constituencies. Through the evaluation process, it is possible to examine what is in place to address concerns and the impact of said policies and procedures.

In some human services agencies, policy language regarding hiring and promotion has been changed to include experiences with cultural and linguistic diversity as a core competency. Health care, high-tech, and insurance companies have broadened their health care policies to include individuals not previously covered, for example, individuals with adult dependents, in same-sex relationships, or in nontraditional family arrangements. In many respects, these changes reflect behaviors in society at large regarding families and relationships.

An evaluation should provide subjective and objective feedback. Diversity initiatives focus on the interface of people and organizational systems, and it follows that evaluations must be balanced, providing both personal and objective data. Subjective or personal data can be gathered through both qualitative and quantitative methods. Subjective feedback, usually based on self-reports by individuals, including employees, instructors, and consultants, relies on perceptions or impressions, opinions, and experiences. This is a similar procedure to that applied in the needs assessment part of the initiative. Objective feedback typically emerges through the use of multiple choice, yes/no, or Likert-type scales. In this case, individuals are provided with a possible range of responses rather than generating their own. Has communication improved in the facility. A range of numerical responses (1-5) or phrases ("strongly agree" to "strongly disagree") could be provided. Objective protocols yield responses that are more readily quantifiable. Responses or scores can be computed for some type of statistical result.

Practical and *timely* are key criteria when considering an assessment. Assessments must measure what was intended to be different or have changed. For example, if a marketing strategy was designed to improve business with a Chinese American community, an assessment could target the increase in the number of purchases made by these clients, not necessarily the items or amount of the purchase. Practically speaking, this methodology to measure units of purchase would become baseline data quickly indicating any change based on the intervention. Timing is also important. Some strategies take a longer time to be realized. To be realistic, evaluations may need to distinguish between short- and long-term strategies and be designed to measure both. It is important here to recognize that trying a new strategy once and not getting the desirable change is not a sufficient reason to eliminate it. Rather, this situation could be seen as a call to examine other conditions surrounding the strategy.

Types of Evaluation

Diversity management initiatives require regular, systematic review, and as the previous discussion has indicated, the mind-set and plans to measure change must give vision to this knowledge-building endeavor. Although I advocate for the development of an evaluation process at the times goals and objectives are being established, I can only cite the nonprofit institutions and a manufacturing facility that have taken this approach proactively. In this discussion, nevertheless, I outline the types of evaluations that can support a diversity initiative. The three types are formative, summative, and intervention specific.

Formative evaluations are designed for assessment at particular points in a multiyear project. With a 3- to 5-year strategic plan, for example, formative evaluations would occur minimally on an annual basis. The goal here is to determine the short-term progress of the initiative. What is changing and why? Who is being affected and why? There are various techniques to uncover this feedback. These might include surveys, discussion groups, or other measures of the stated goals and objectives. In my evaluation experiences, I have assisted organizations in gathering baseline data that can be referenced against the original findings of a cultural audit. For example, a museum I worked with was concerned with low attendance by residents of ethnic and racial minority backgrounds who lived in neighboring towns. Through a needs assessment, museum staff identified workplace appearance as unreflective of the culturally diverse community surrounding them. Through a short-term intervention, they were able to inventory building space and determine the types of new artifacts and reading materials that might be purchased. This action responded to an identified concern but also became another example of institutionalization. Over the next 1 to 3 years, they tracked the rates of admission by all new visitors. Through this approach, they were able to document increases in visits by the residents they had targeted as well.

Summative evaluations assess the end product(s). Using a broad-based approach, this type of evaluation makes a comprehensive assessment of a multiyear initiative. It measures both general and specific areas of change. I have conducted summative evaluations for numerous change-oriented projects that had specific time-limited goals and interventions. For example, with federal funding, social services agencies have designed educational programs to reduce teenage pregnancy. Typically, funding is designated for a period of time. At the termination of the project, a summative evaluation is expected.

I have not been asked to carry out summative evaluations for diversity initiatives thus far. I attribute this to the relative newness of diversity initiatives in the workplace; the fact that initiatives are designed to introduce multilevel, multistrategy-based change over a period of time; and assumptions that eventually diversity-driven strategies will become integrated into the systems and operational behavior of an organization.

It is important to keep in mind that formative and summative evaluations are based on the initiative's goals and objectives. They must test the efficacy of the strategies that support the goals. For example, in a number of work settings, sexual harassment and gender bias emerge as concerns. To address these, a specific goal regarding workplace climate is usually established: to create a respectful work environment. This would be followed by different strategies specifically designed to address sexual harassment and gender bias. At the time of an evaluation, various measures for change could be tested: (a) fewer complaints by women of patronizing feedback and sexist assignments from their supervisors, (b) fewer incidents of sexual harassment or the reverse, (c) feedback that indicates that the work environment feels safer and more comfortable, and (d) increased responsiveness by management to complaints.

Through this example, I demonstrate that different measures of change are possible. In my work with diversity committees and planners, it has been possible to generate numerous behavioral indicators of change regarding each goal and objective.

Intervention-specific evaluations typically occur at the end of a particular activity designed to promote change. This activity could be a training session, an event, or some other type of intervention. The purpose of this evaluation is twofold: to determine how in content and process the intervention supports and carries out an initiative's objectives, and to gather a new type of baseline data, specifically relating to training programs.

At the end of the training sessions I lead, for example, an evaluation is always done. This gives the trainers feedback about their performance, provides information about the relevance of the training, indicates whether initiative objectives are being effectively addressed through the training, and allows participants to reflect on what they learned. This range of feedback can lead to a redesign of the program and provoke thinking about other types of training and what material is impacting participants positively or adversely.

Intervention-specific evaluations should be viewed as one part of a comprehensive evaluation process. The data they provide can inform, reshape, and reinforce other tasks and processes that are meant to support the organization's goals for diversity.

Diversity management interventions are designed to introduce positive change that impacts individuals and the organization as a whole. Consequently, evaluation procedures must be applied at all levels.

Methodology and Procedures

Many of the same comments about methodology and procedures described in Chapter 5 can be made here. Clarification about the quantitative and qualitative approach, the types of instruments or other formats used to gather data, and the analyses to be performed all require decisions. Perhaps the most important distinction between the needs assessment (audit) and evaluation is the focus of the evaluation on assessing change and impact. The audit is a process to identify concerns and create baseline indices for later measurement.

QUANTIFYING DATA

I continue to hear a great deal of emphasis on quantifying the impact of diversity initiatives. In a number of organizations, there are specific inquiries about productivity measures in relation to financial results. Planners believe that because of the deliberate investment of resources into diversity initiatives, evidence of return on the dollar should manifest. To measure productivity is no small undertaking. It requires a complex methodology called econometrics. In utilizing this approach, various data are required to answer the question about productivity. One must explore interpersonal behavior, systems, and other factors that impact the business. For example, if downsizing occurs in the midst of the diversity initiative, this event and its effects would have to be factored into the productivity measurement process. Are people producing more because they do not want to lose their jobs? Is productivity down because individuals are preoccupied about their work future? It would be very difficult to isolate these phenomena when evaluating the impact of diversity management. My advice to planners who want to quantify change is that it can be done, provided a long-term time line and logical process are followed. Furthermore, consultants with expertise in econometrics would be essential.

QUALITATIVE MEASURES

As in the needs assessment process, qualitative approaches make it possible to gather information about change as perceived and experienced by different organizational stakeholders. Again, focus groups and interviews are the primary methods.

Areas of inquiry of course reflect strategic goals. These might include sense of comfort and respect with coworkers and management, access to information about career ladders within the organization and support for career planning, sense of inclusion even though one is different from the "majority" workforce, access to accurate and timely information needed to accomplish one's tasks, and the use of performance evaluations that are fair and appropriate.

In some ways, it might seem that yes or no responses could be provided about these goals, but the purpose for using qualitative methods is to obtain discussions that allow for descriptive information and anecdotes about the area of inquiry. Because diversity initiatives are highly focused on people as critical to the organization's goals, it is essential to learn how individuals experience new strategies and policies that are intended to support them.

Additional qualitative data can come through observations by diversity management personnel. Because of their proximity to the initiative's goals, they might be able to report about the cooperation, or lack thereof they are receiving from management in the implementation strategy, changes in communication patterns (e.g., access to particular power brokers), and the level of comfort versus tension that is present when groups such as the diversity committee meet. One diversity director described having a feeling of walking on eggshells whenever conversation focused on differences of gender and race. His hope was that over time these conversations could be held with greater comfort and ease. In focus groups, participants can articulate their experiences in this regard as well as their perceptions about the usefulness of different diversity strategies.

Where permanent changes are introduced through the development or refinement of policies and procedures, qualitative inquiry can determine how the changes contribute to work-family balance or how the redistribution of workload eases stress and contributes to productivity. In one manufacturing facility, a new job-posting process was instituted to provide greater access to interested parties. Through the evaluation focus group, it was possible to explore whether greater access was being realized, whether employees were actually participating in the new process, and what other steps could be taken to make the posting process user friendly.

In a human services agency, existing polices regarding layoffs and termination were suspended during a reorganization process. This allowed the director to retain ethnic- and racial-minority personnel who lacked seniority but reflected the clients served. By exercising this option, the agency board demonstrated leadership, supported its mission and goals for diversity, responded to existing needs related to clients of color, and also reinforced organizational goals for staff diversity.

Use of Consultants for Evaluation

Evaluation of a diversity management initiative typically involves use of an outside consultant or team of consultants. This occurs in part because high-quality evaluation requires specialized research skills and experience that salaried staff of an organization often do not possess. In addition and perhaps just as important, the objectivity provided by an outside party can be an important factor in ensuring credibility of findings.

The purpose of this brief section is to examine issues associated with involvement of consultants for evaluation of diversity management initiatives, including suggestions to ensure their optimal use. It should be noted that the participation of consultants for program evaluation is a subset of the use of consultants in general, and all of the concepts and suggestions offered in Chapter 2 also apply here. At the same time, consultants for evaluation introduce additional issues and requirements, which I examine in three general areas: (a) preparation for use of the consultant, (b) recruitment of the consultant and establishment of a contract, and (c) the roles played by the consultant. In each area examples are described and suggestions are offered.

PRELIMINARY ACTIVITIES

Most organizations make some preparations prior to recruiting and selecting consultants for evaluation of a diversity project, although some make more thorough and comprehensive preparations than do others. In general, those organizations that pay more careful attention to these important underpinnings and preliminary activities tend to be more satisfied with their consultants and also achieve more of their evaluation objectives. The following are particularly important prerequisites and preparations for use of consultants in this evaluation process.

Formulate Clear Goals and Measurable Objectives. Clear goals and measurable objectives are vital. As described above, the starting point for virtually every evaluation is the goals and objectives of the project being evaluated. The formulation of clear project goals and measurable objectives is essential to a successful evaluation and provides a solid basis for planning the evaluation.

Plan for Evaluation From the Start. Very often, evaluations are begun long after an initiative is under way, in many cases shortly before the project is scheduled to "end" (not necessarily with diversity management initiatives). It may be natural to think of evaluation as something to be done after a project has already been started, but organizations that plan for evaluation right from the start tend to be more satisfied. There are several advantages to an early start, including improved diversity direction; planning based on clear goals and measurable objectives; useful feedback to the diversity director, committee, and managers throughout the life of the project rather than just at the end; and measurement of change over the entire life of the initiative.

Involve Evaluator(s) Early. Not only is it useful to plan for evaluation from the start, it also is useful to involve the evaluator(s) from near the beginning. By early involvement, the evaluator(s) can help provide an effective plan to ensure that the project itself has clear goals and measurable objectives and that these are focused and feasible. In addition, early involvement allows for integration of the evaluation into the project itself, making it more efficient, less costly, and likely to yield more useful and valid information.

Collect Data From the Start. Building an evaluation from the beginning allows for collection of data from the beginning of the initiative project and continuing throughout its life, providing a solid basis for measurement of change over time. This is a very important element in a comprehensive evaluation that typically is not possible if the evaluation does not start until late in a project. In addition, collection of data from the start provides useful feedback to project managers throughout the life of the project and not just at the end, leading to useful program modifications and refinements while the project is in progress. For example, one can view the diversity assessment process described in an earlier chapter of this book as the establishment of baseline data for the evaluation of the project, with subsequent periodic data collection throughout the life of the project intended to measure change on key variables associated with achievement of project objectives over time.

RECRUITMENT AND CONTRACTING

The processes of recruiting and contracting with evaluation consultants also bear some examination. Based on my experience, certain aspects of these processes appear to be associated with greater success with consultants. Qualifications to look for in a consultant or team of consultants to assist in evaluation of diversity management initiatives include

- ❏ Skills and prior experience with evaluation: In choosing consultants to assist with evaluation, consultants with substantial, formal, social science research skills and extensive prior hands-on experience conducting evaluations are likely to be most effective and successful. In this regard, experience with a wide variety of types of research methods and projects is desirable.
- ❏ Experience with diversity: Consultants with a lot of previous experience doing consultation in the area of diversity are most likely to be successful.
- ❏ Cultural or racial minority status: Although not an absolute requirement, I believe it is desirable to include consultants from multiple cultural and racial backgrounds on the evaluation team for diversity management projects. Consultants who have more direct personal understanding of

the issues under study are helpful in keeping an evaluation on target and add depth and subtlety to analysis and interpretation of findings.

❑ Openness and flexibility: Openness and flexibility are important qualities in any consultant. Consultants who are perceived as lacking these qualities tend to be less effective.

❑ Fit with agency: Although intangible, fit seems to be quite important. It is wise to learn enough about a consultant's style and approach to be able to judge whether or not he or she will fit into the agency's culture.

Several factors are important in the area of review and contracting for successful use of consultants:

❑ Committee involvement: Those agencies in which there is substantial involvement of a diversity committee or several members of the organization in the identification and selection of the evaluation consultant or team, including review of proposals and interviews, tend to work best. Extensive involvement apparently increases ownership of the process and helps to ensure acceptability of the consultant.

❑ Written RFP: Use of a written request for proposal (RFP) is desirable, including clear statements of project goals and objectives, expected consultant activities, and qualifications. In this regard, it is appropriate and desirable to request information about prior evaluations conducted by the consultants, copies of completed evaluation reports, and names and phone numbers of organizations for whom the consultant(s) performed past evaluations as references.

❑ Written bid: Submission of written bids by prospective consultants or consulting groups is desirable.

❑ Technical review: Because the written bids are likely to include technical research designs and methods, it may be desirable to ask a qualified independent researcher to review and comment on the technical merit of proposals by bidders.

❑ Written contract and work plan: Finally, when a consultant has been selected, a clear written contract, including a work schedule and products, is an important mechanism to ensure clear understanding of the work as well as accountability.

ROLE OF CONSULTANTS IN EVALUATION

In this section, I examine the several roles and functions performed by outside consultants in evaluation of diversity management initiatives, with suggestions to facilitate effectiveness.

Joint Planning and Implementation. In my experience, evaluations are most successful when the outside evaluation consultants work jointly with representatives of the project under study to plan and carry out the evaluation. Rather than expecting the outside consultants to carry out the evaluation independently, joint planning and implementation has a number of benefits, including procedures to ensure the evaluation is tailored to the specific needs and interests of the organization's management, a sense of joint ownership and interest in the findings, and the flexibility to modify the evaluation in progress to accommodate shifting priorities and needs.

Evaluation Consultant as Technical Expert. It is useful to view the evaluator as a kind of technical expert with specialized knowledge in a number of areas, including research design; sampling; design and selection of measurement instruments; data collection, data entry, and statistical analysis; focus group methodology; and the like. In the joint planning and implementation of the evaluation, the primary role of the evaluation consultant is to identify the most reliable and valid methods to answer the evaluation questions posed by the representatives of the client organization and to carry out or oversee activities to answer the questions.

External Versus Internal Evaluation. Evaluations can be viewed as varying along a continuum from entirely external evaluations, which are planned and carried out exclusively by outside evaluators, to purely internal evaluations, which are planned and carried out entirely by staff of an organization without any help from outside consultants. In actual practice, most evaluations fall somewhere in between the extremes to accommodate the specific requirements of each situation, and it is useful to weigh carefully in advance the extent to which an evaluation should rely on external versus internal resources. At least two factors are important in making this decision:

1. *Time frame:* When the time frame for the evaluation is short and information is needed quickly and on a one-time-only basis, then typically an external evaluation planned and carried out primarily by outside consultants is the only alternative. Outside consultants already skilled in the necessary methods can carry out the evaluation and

deliver the findings on a timely basis. When the time frame is long term and information will be needed periodically on a routine basis over time, then development of internal evaluation systems within the organization itself may be more appropriate. In this case, there is time for the internal training and capacity building that may be necessary, and the internal evaluation systems may allow greater internal control at less cost over time than would an external evaluation.

2. *Need for objectivity:* In general, when issues under study are controversial and the various parties involved in a project being evaluated are at odds over its effectiveness and value, then an external evaluation probably is desirable. Often, external evaluators are viewed as more objective and credible because they do not have vested interests in the outcome of the evaluation. On the other hand, in situations where information being collected is not controversial and all parties agree on the meaning and value of the information, then internal evaluation systems to collect and report information may be more efficient and useful.

In practice, not only do most evaluations fall somewhere between the two extremes, but some start out as primarily external evaluations and then move toward primarily internal evaluations as internal capacities are developed, making the outside consultants less necessary.

Summary: Learning Through Evaluations

It has been my privilege to have been asked to assist with different stages and processes in diversity initiatives. Introducing an evaluation, in my experience, has always been accompanied by trepidation about what might be found. Even for organizations seemingly implementing planned and responsive strategies, questions about whether there has, in fact, been any change still abound. My evaluations have yielded rich data. These can be grouped into three main areas: evidence of progress and permanent change, factors and pitfalls to success, and unintentional effects of the diversity management initiative.

The data that support these categories are best understood in the context of a particular organization's goals and objectives and the application of both quantitative and qualitative methodology. At the same time, I have learned similar lessons across different environments, suggesting to me some of the generic features of change-oriented strategies and processes.

By design, diversity management initiatives promote individual and organizational change. Evaluations are the best vehicle to learn about progress, success, and errors. I can think of too many examples where 2- to 3-year projects were not formally reviewed or assessed. Specific interventions were evaluated, but there was no master plan for the entire initiative. Tremendous valuable data is lost as a result. There are many lessons about people, systems, and the organizational culture that can be derived through the evaluation of a diversity initiative. In the long run, the entire organization can benefit.

Guidelines for Evaluating Progress and Change

1. Think of evaluations as a strategy to assess change and impact.
2. Build in an evaluation strategy from the start.
3. Think of evaluations as instruments for knowledge building and future planning.
4. An evaluation requires a plan of action with a stated purpose, methodology, and expected outcome.
5. Measure progress against stated goals and objectives.
6. Make evaluation procedures inclusive of all constituencies in the organization.
7. Use both qualitative and quantitative procedures to assess change.
8. Make inquiries at macro and micro levels.
9. Seek evidence of permanent change(s).
10. Expect three types of findings: desirable, undesirable, and unexpected.
11. Do not view lack of change as failure. Rather, consider exploring other contextual factors.
12. Realize that diversity management occurs in the context of multiple forces. Change likely results from a combination of deliberate strategies and indirect factors.
13. Select consultants who can guide the evaluation process.

10

Identifying Enablers and Pitfalls for Diversity Initiatives

❑ What enables an initiative to move smoothly?
❑ What might be barriers along the way?
❑ How will resistances manifest?
❑ Can pitfalls be anticipated rather than come as surprises?

❑ Roosevelt Thomas, author of *Beyond Race and Gender* (1991), refers to today's business environment as "permanent white-water," manifesting conditions that require ever-present flexibility and adaptability to a myriad of conditions. Diversity initiatives could be described similarly. Because they are organic and evolving processes and require movement into uncharted territory, they are affected by any number of forces and factors. In society, there is a mixed chorus of supporters and opponents of diversity-related efforts. In some organizations, an initiative is greeted warmly. Often, the words of managers go something like this: "An overwhelming number of our managers are intellectually honest and like to think of themselves as unbiased, and this helps their support of action strategies." In other organizations, perceptions about favoritism to certain individuals and groups, "reverse discrimination," as it is called, can create a backlash to diversity initiatives.

Within organizations, an initiative is affected by leadership, different constituencies, operational systems, policies and practices, and external factors. Together and independently, these push an initiative forward or impede it. And throughout all phases of my blueprint for planning and managing diversity initiatives, an organization experiences high and low points, challenges, and enablers. Can these be anticipated in advance or are they simply inevitable?

My study of more than 50 agencies and cultural institutions experienced in diversity initiatives introduced me to a number of factors that can be both enablers and obstacles to these change-oriented processes. In addition, my work as a consultant has provided a bird's-eye view of factors that support or obstruct goals of the diversity management process. Interviews with the organizational leaders of initiatives introduce other examples and experiences. All of these data provide rich clues and guidance for diversity planners and leaders. Although each organization has a different culture, there are still similarities when a highly visible process of change is introduced. In this chapter, I discuss enablers and obstacles, concluding with a section on what organizational agents report they might have done differently. Learning from others' difficulties and successes does not mean all pitfalls can be avoided. Minimally, however, leaders of a diversity initiative should have a chance to sidestep more than a few problems.

Enablers

As might be expected, there are different types of enablers, some more predictable than others and some essential to the progress and ultimate success of an initiative. I break the enablers into four broad categories: essentials, organizational culture and practices, people, and external factors. Not surprising, some of these enablers also emerge as barriers.

ESSENTIALS

1. A clear, holistic definition of diversity and diversity management, and the creation of an organizational business case are primary starting points for an initiative. As one diversity leader put it, "Defining diversity is key because the dynamics of diversity are real. In our organization, we defined it to include all people and all of our issues. For example, there are young couples with dual careers, salary differentials, and relocations. All of these people concerns are business related as well. Describing diversity this way—by example—automatically makes it a business issue."

A university spokesperson reported, "Diversity was addressed before it became a visible business issue. Our location in the city historically abutting multicultural and low-income neighborhoods meant we were always trying to actualize our mission of access to higher education for disenfranchised groups, from the Irish to today's population of persons of color. Defining diversity in terms of business and education goals came quite naturally for us."

Most of the organizational leaders I have worked with agree that defining diversity as a business imperative is a more effective way to reach different constituencies within their business. "We see it as an imperative to profitability. We need to be able to draw on the diversity of our customer base and at the same time provide accessible services to them, whether they are senior citizens or foreign students attending a local university," reported a bank executive. "This may mean different outreach, products, and practices to accommodate the customer, but we cannot do it without an infrastructure of personnel and other systems to capitalize on this market." These are essentials.

Social services agencies and educational institutions have traditionally described diversity management as a social and moral responsibility. Delivery of human services primarily to a public that is urban or cannot afford private care has long depended on external funding from governmental entities, foundations, and corporations. Reductions in funding, changes in the health care and insurance systems, and an increase in operational costs have led these organizations to redefine the rationale and definition of diversity. "It is about social and business responsibility as well," stated the director of one multiservice agency. "We have had to broaden our thinking and that of many social workers as well. Before, to talk about our work as 'business' did not occur. It sounded too capitalistic. If we do not think about what we do in business terms, our very existence is threatened."

A definition of diversity and diversity management *in business terms* is essential to a successful initiative. There has to be a way of demonstrating the relationship between organizational viability and a diversity plan for success. All of this takes us back to the discussion in Chapter 3. Recognizing and communicating motivating factors through a business rationale for the organization gives diversity management the credibility and visibility it requires.

2. The *process* of the initiative, how well it is thought out, planned, and managed, is also essential to progress and success. In a number of settings, I have seen organizational leaders involve themselves and others in understanding as much as possible about the field of diversity management. They spoke to other companies and diversity directors, read related materials, and benchmarked. "We had discussions about diversity among the three initiative leaders for about 4 to 5 months. We wanted to understand what we were getting into," said a hospital administrator. A museum director said, "We began a formal process 4 years ago, but I guess you could say we were planning and preparing a few years prior to that. It all started to take shape by using a multidivisional and multilevel committee from the beginning."

Some of my interviewees talked about experiencing false starts that led them to redirect their plan. Others acknowledged that they had no specific road map to follow, but that deliberate preparation and planning enabled a smoother process. According to the diversity director of a regional insurance firm, good thinking and planning allowed him to work from his original plan for 2 full years. "I took a quality approach using a diversity overlay to begin to change the culture of our firm. I developed and followed a flow chart that enabled moving forward with the process of the initiative." The diversity vice president of a manufacturing company reported, "I knew it was going to be challenging so I did as much prereading and discussing with different consultants as possible. It helped."

3. Having the initiative supported at the top has consistently been cited as an identifiable enabler by individuals I spoke with. "Without a doubt, support of the CEO and senior vice president has been the

greatest enabler," one initiative leader reported. CEOs or executives who give an initiative their imprimatur and leadership—in action, not just words—reportedly make a big difference not just for the initiative but for the individual(s) designated to manage the process. "We had senior management support but also the autonomy to do the work," one interviewee said. Others talked about upper-level support and leadership as the catalyst and most-effective enabler of the process. "Executive management realized that expectations had been raised and therefore they had to move forward," a bank manager observed.

4. The knowledge and credibility of the diversity director is also essential to enabling the necessary outreach, planning, and directing an initiative requires. "A rookie cannot do this kind of job," reported a seasoned diversity director with international experience. "You have to recognize organizational politics and be astute enough not to let them become obstacles." Persons with more seniority, interdisciplinary experiences, and excellent work performance are harder to discredit, according to my research. Organizational planners with real-life experiences of difference, not considered "traditional" managers, were also favored as initiative leaders. Morrison et al. (1993) refer to white women and persons of color eligible for these positions as *nontraditional managers*. "Any diversity director needs to understand how to use power in the organization and what it means to her or him personally. A lot of hot buttons can easily be pushed," said one leader. All of those I interviewed agreed that a diversity leader has to be "highly visible" on a repeated basis. One strong show of support is not enough. In the words of one initiative leader, "When you orchestrate the process, then you directly and indirectly make things happen. Going public and drawing in the CEO and other power brokers early on establishes an important message for the organization."

5. Accurate, well-timed, multilevel communication processes leave less room for misunderstanding and create more visibility. In the words of one interviewee, "People know something is going on. Rather than have them guess, we try to get the message out through senior vice presidents and their direct reports. It has to work its way down through the organization." Another diversity leader used the monthly company newsletter to communicate progress through two regular

awareness-building columns. One he wrote, and the other column was written by an employee on a diversity-related theme.

As an initiative unfolds, different means can be used to communicate about its progress. At a museum, multilingual programs and announcements about exhibits and other services were used. A number of organizations I worked with developed diversity brochures in the second or third year of their initiative and disseminated these to all employees. This gave both voice and visibility to the diversity business goals.

6. Committees, councils, or advisory groups were mentioned by all organizations as an essential element in the planning and implementation of their initiative. "Having a committee in place from the beginning supported the slow and meticulous process of creating an infrastructure for change," reported a diversity committee member. One firm established a *Workforce 2000* committee that met on a monthly basis to support, develop, and empower the diversity director. A vice president credited the formation of an advisory committee comprising senior managers of various operating units as giving the initiative the impetus it needed. He reports, "They gave strategic direction from the beginning and because of their senior roles of power, they were able to influence the actions of resisters."

One hospital turned a semidefunct affirmative action committee into a diversity council. The new focus on organizational change through diversity energized past and new participants. "Their charge, now that the process is under way, is to be a sounding board, staying tuned to people issues and planning social and educational activities."

ORGANIZATIONAL CULTURE

The values, norms, and practices of an organization are strong forces at play during the course of a diversity management initiative. The dominant status quo represented by individuals, business units, departments, and other environmental forces will challenge and be challenged by a proactive diversity initiative. And although organizational culture may seem to be set in stone rather than fluid, there are still enabling criteria from the culture that can support the progress of an initiative:

An Open, Participatory Versus Paternalistic Management Approach. If employees actively participate with management on teams or committees to work on common concerns, value is given to everyone's input. "Access to senior management in these forums can be a positive precipitant and certainly helped when it came to the diversity initiative," said one person I interviewed.

Where there is openness, more issues can be discussable. When people first learn about an organizational focus on diversity, they respond in different ways. Some immediately balk, labeling it political correctness and seeing it as too much trouble or a program only for women and persons of color. "There is denial, concern that something's wrong, and a sense of self-defense might set in. Some of this is normal, because people naturally resist change, however. You cannot do this work with a sledgehammer," said one experienced initiative leader. "There has to be a certain kind of sensibility and good judgment in helping people to understand the whys of a diversity initiative." In an organizational culture where a number of the essentials are in place and where there is a sense of openness, questions can be raised and challenges made without fear. Dialogue and effective communication are key enablers to demystifying diversity management.

A Learning-Oriented Environment Where Education Is Promoted and Linked to Continuous Improvement and Productivity. Empowering people through training, recognition, and rewards makes a difference when it comes to initiating diversity-related strategies. With this type of environment, an initiative may be more readily perceived as another learning opportunity, a topic with a direct relationship to job performance, relevant to current business priorities, and an indication of the organization's thinking about the future. Quite often, individuals want to know what they are going to get from the initiative. In my experience, demonstration and participation through learning-based activities make concepts come to life, enabling individuals to better recognize their personal benefits from different strategies.

At an insurance company, diversity site councils at various office locations were charged with making recommendations for educational programs. In a manufacturing facility, a quality and diversity initiative were integrated. The educational programs that resulted were designed to promote themes of awareness and respect, underpinnings of their continuous improvement process.

A mentoring project involving 10 company officers was used by one organization to educate everyone involved in the initiative. These officers needed to know the diversity business case and also had to be proactive with the committees they led. They were not only champions for the initiative but by their leadership were guides for individuals who volunteered to serve on the committee. "By labeling it a mentoring opportunity, we were able to give an example of a concept that is highly touted but not always put into practice, certainly not as it related to diversity management," noted a bank executive.

Demonstrated Efforts to Create a Representative Workforce. Most organizations, for profit and not for profit, are headed by middle-aged white males. This is a historical fact that continues to occur, but in response to Johnston and Packer's (1987) *Workforce 2000* projections, affirmative action, and federal guidelines promulgated under Title VII of the Civil Rights Act of 1964 to prevent discrimination in employment based on color, race, religion, sex, and national origin, many workplaces have stepped up their efforts to recruit, hire, and promote white women and persons of color. The Americans With Disabilities Act of 1990; company policies that apply to heterosexual and homosexual individuals and their families; and other initiatives that address typically disenfranchised employees such as older workers, immigrant employees, and others have emerged or taken on a greater presence as organizations attempt to address representation in their workforce. Deliberate strategies to have a broader-based, demographically distinctive workforce sends a positive message that supports the initiative. For example, job fairs in community-based agencies or business-related booths at ethnic-specific events have been strategies to attract underrepresented individuals.

Accountability That Is Shared by Different Forces Behind the Initiative. Diversity-related strategies driven by business units and departments lead to expectations about accountability. In one health care system, vice presidents had a mandate for themselves as well as all of their direct reports. This systemic but decentralized approach has been described in organizational management texts as the recommended route to follow to introduce change. In his study of businesses, Michael Beer and his colleagues (Beer, Eistenstat, & Spector, 1990) found that giving departments the autonomy to plan and deliver their own change strategies yields results faster.

In larger corporate entities with multiple sites and comprehensive operating units, decentralization is essential. To implement the initiative throughout the company, site administrators or directors are charged with facilitating the process. "The initiative has to be woven into the fabric of the agency so that it becomes everyone's responsibility," one diversity leader said. A bank executive added, "The diversity initiative needs to be more systemic, linked to all facets of the business so that eventually diversity-driven strategies become institutionalized."

Of course, accompanying a decentralized approach must be educational interventions to guide the work. Those charged with developing their unit's diversity plan must have guidance and collaboration with the diversity director or committee to design an appropriate plan. To assign such an important business task without appropriate preparation is a setup for failure for the individual expected to demonstrate accountability.

A Willingness to Measure Change. A number of diversity directors with more than 3 years of diversity leadership experience spoke of the need to assess progress and change. "In our company, we had the senior management team draft an action plan for areas of concern. They set objectives and enabling strategies, and projected possible behavioral indicators of change. This task got them to think critically about what might change and the benefits that could accrue with respect to business practices. I think they were surprised about what might result," said a human resources manager active in her company's diversity initiative.

All of the more than 50 human services and cultural institutions I was involved with had an evaluation task built into their process as recommended in Chapter 9. "This helped to create a mind-set that we were looking for change and other results. It was more than doing the right thing or being politically correct," said an agency director. "Our cultural audits identified issues and concerns, and we had to find ways to address them. I think some of the bank executives were pleasantly surprised when we were able to document how some of our strategies had addressed the concerns. There were slight changes, such as including persons of color in the pool of attorneys who handle closings and creating a handbook describing standards for language in the workplace." "This handbook was a tool to business efficiency," noted the diversity director. "Furthermore, these data gave support to the initiative, its progress and benefits."

PEOPLE

It has already been stated that expressed commitment by senior management is an essential enabler to an initiative. But there are other individuals and groups who can move the process along. In some instances, leaders look to the way other new initiatives are promoted within their organization. In one bank, diversity leadership teams were formed, one for each business line. Their charge was to develop an action plan for each of the areas requiring attention. Accountability went back to the bank's executive policy group, which received reports on a quarterly basis.

Boards of directors, overseers, or trustees have been described as another enabling constituency. In all nonprofit organizations I have worked with or talked to, the board's understanding of issues, willingness to engage in the diversity management planning and implementation process, and visible leadership were strong enablers. A museum representative mentioned earlier that the trustees participated on the diversity committee giving it a high level of regard. At their annual meeting, the same board involved community residents in sociocultural activities. At a family services agency, board members realized that they needed to model the change through their own behavior, participating in diversity training, supporting new work and family policies, and reading about other human services diversity work. This visible and proactive demonstration signaled to staff that the organization was shifting gears and the responsibility was being assumed by the board as well.

Employees in general were cited in all workplaces as key enablers to the success of an initiative. "Middle management saw this as a way of getting more productivity and to promote and empower people. This in turn would reflect positively on them." At an insurance company, employees applied to serve on the first diversity committee.

"Their willingness and enthusiasm, and the fact that they were all different individuals gave the initiative a positive start." A museum established change teams and advocates to help to carry out the goals of the strategic plan. These teams of multilevel employees and volunteers brought a richness of perspectives and experience to bear on the areas the initiative targeted for change. "The change teams were charged to create an institution that reflects and serves the broadest public. Their collective voices, not always in agreement, were able to support the mission of the museum," the diversity coordinator said proudly.

EXTERNAL ENABLERS

Demographic trends, national projections, and local realities have also been identified by initiative leaders as enablers, provided the organization views them with the mind-set that the glass is half full, not half empty. It was reported by those I interviewed that although demographic projections can seem overwhelming, they need to be viewed as a reality and factored into an organization's strategic planning process. The diversity director of an insurance company says he likes to remind business leaders that the buying power of immigrants and persons of color in 1995 is estimated at $600 billion. "Some of this capital is in our backyard. We have to develop strategies to reach it." The executive director of an ad foundation also asserts that the industry has much to gain and give by taking these data into consideration.

Mind-set can be a problem in some organizations, noted a medical director. "People hear the demographics and think they have to run out and interview scores of white women and persons of color. I want them to stop and think about these numbers of people as opportunities for the organization," he said.

Too often recruiters and managers get hung up on the term *qualified*, stated a diversity director of a financial institution. "This becomes a mental barrier in carrying out their task. Instead, they should think differently, think about the skill sets that are needed in the future workplace. If peoples' skill sets meet the business needs, then it is a match. The language targeting 'qualified' to white women and people of color, not white men, then becomes irrelevant."

Emerging markets, particularly globally, are also referred to as an external force. Rosabeth Kanter (1995) describes globalization as "one of the most powerful and pervasive influences on nations, businesses, workplaces, communities, and lives at the end of the twentieth century" (p. 11). For all organizations, this may already be a reality. Foreign nationals come here on assignment and Americans go to other parts of the world. Bilingual and multicultural competence become priorities in a global business environment.

Competition was continuously mentioned by those I spoke with as an external driver of a diversity initiative. In the business world, there is increasing pressure to hire desirable talent, and this means being in the position to be an employer of choice. In focus groups with white women, persons of color, and gay and lesbian employees, awareness about this issue was repeatedly raised. Some individuals believe they can be selective and assess the suitability of a future employer. Organizational status in this regard is supported by both positive and negative press as well as by communication through informal grapevines.

Competition is also discussed in terms of market share. All of the diversity directors and vice presidents, whether in human services, education, or corporate environments, underscored their awareness about the marketplace. "We don't have to go overseas to find diversity. It comes in many forms in our catchment area. It is up to us to find ways to reach the people," reported a health center administrator. The advertising industry is also aware of the need to establish niche markets to pursue consumers who historically have been ignored.

The advertising industry is also aware of the need to pursue niche markets based on a specific type of demographic diversity that has historically been ignored. Nowadays, advertisements by major businesses such as Sears, McDonald's, and General Motors are commonplace in women's, senior citizen, and ethnic- and race-specific publications. In addition, some organizations with deliberate plans to support workforce diversity may seek evidence that an advertising firm has representative personnel working on their account.

Consultants were identified as both enablers and barriers to a diversity initiative by those I spoke with, seeming to confirm my comments in Chapters 2 and 9. Those who reported success spoke of having defined clear roles for consultants. The director of diversity for a health insurance carrier underscored the importance of working with a good consultant along the way. "This person can keep you level headed, help you to maintain some objectivity when your balance gets thrown off." Others spoke of consultants as persons skilled in organizational development strategies, individuals who understand the impact of change strategies on the equilibrium of an organization. "If you are looking for a trainer that's one thing, but if you want a strategist, a 'big picture' thinker, that's something else," noted a diversity coordinator. She also highlighted the need to develop a partnership approach with consultants. "It's important that both parties realize that we are working toward the same goals."

SUMMARY

All organizational personnel I have worked with would agree that a combination of enabling factors moves the process of an initiative forward. These people advocate a comprehensive approach, beginning with a clear definition and business rationale for diversity, and a strategic, long-term perspective. Thoughtful leadership, involvement across multiple levels of an organization, and clear statements of what was expected from different constituencies and what could be reasonably accomplished in the short and long term were also identified as key elements to the success of an initiative. Diversity directors I have interviewed see themselves as change agents but readily admit that an initiative is not the job or responsibility of one person. Finally, accountability was highlighted regularly by those I queried, accountability on the part of senior management *and* the entire organization. As one diversity director put it, "The leadership and modeling must come from the top of the house."

Barriers

Barriers come in many forms and present themselves at different stages of a diversity initiative. Some are readily identifiable before an initiative gets under way; others emerge en route. The challenge is to recognize, not avoid them, and be prepared to keep a clear head to deal with them. The barriers to the initiative described below fall into three categories: the initiative itself, the organizational culture, and human elements.

THE INITIATIVE ITSELF

Quite often, diversity initiatives are unreasonably expected to address long-standing, unresolved issues that affect workplace productivity, employee satisfaction, and changes in the customer base. Viewing an initiative as a dumping ground for complaints or treating it like Aladdin's magic lamp leads to major disappointments. The initiative needs to be viewed as a *process,* I heard repeatedly from interviewees. "What we are doing is trying to change organizational culture and by consequence alter the environment. This is a long-term, complicated challenge. Diversity directors have to be clear about this and communicate it to their leaders in case they underestimate the complexity. There are no shortcuts," a diversity vice president said emphatically. Being too ambitious and looking for immediate, dramatic results were frequently referred to as barriers to the processes of organizational change.

A lack of clear goals and a well-communicated sense of direction and purpose were also reported as an obstacle to success. As one diversity leader put it, "People need to hear the business reasons a number of times in different ways. Once is not enough."

The majority of diversity leaders I queried agreed that to build an initiative by beginning with training was not a good idea. "I think the training alienated too many people because it was mandatory. Furthermore, the departments had not done any preparation to lay the groundwork for the training. It was just dropped in and viewed as punitive," noted a university director. There were other stories about how training emotionally stirred up participants, leaving many in a state of turmoil and upset. This not only gave training a negative connotation but also damaged the credibility of the initiative. The timing for and purpose of training has to be clear and not confused with the essence of the initiative.

Another obstacle emanating from the initiative itself is the confusion surrounding affirmative action and the failure to distinguish an initiative from it. "If we talk in terms of hirings and promotions only, people hear language that is associated with affirmative action. Perceptions of reverse discrimination result and this can damage the credibility of the initiative," observed a bank executive. "We need to evaluate our effectiveness with affirmative action, see what works and does not work, but not confuse it with diversity management."

THE ORGANIZATIONAL CULTURE

"Creating discomfort, challenging boundaries, and taking a process versus product approach all challenge the status quo," reported the vice president of a global consumer products corporation. "Change is naturally going to cause discomfort, but if a change leader does not understand the culture and subcultures of the organization, she or he may misread or overreact to symptoms of discomfort. Some intervention may be necessary, but you have to know what to do and when."

How work gets done and what gets valued are also manifestations of organizational culture. It is not hard to foresee that when it comes to a diversity initiative, which is naturally less predictable than other business initiatives in terms of quantifiable results, skepticism or demands for cost-effectiveness are often an obstacle to success. "The culture of U.S. companies is task completion and output versus process oriented. The belief is that you can schedule and control your business goals and predict an end point. Quotas are set to produce X number of products or to increase sales by a measurable percentage. Diversity initiatives are not as easily defined," one diversity leader said.

Some organizations, in their zeal to be socially responsible, jump into an initiative as though it were a new product they want to bring to the marketplace before everyone else. This practice does not work well, according to diversity planners I have spoken with. "Failure to do self-examination and to not understand your own self-interest in a diversity initiative can become an obstacle down the road," one interviewee put it. As has been noted earlier, clarification about self-interest, thoughtful preparation, and planning are essentials to a successful process.

Another impediment identified was organizational structure itself. One health center director noted that autonomy among the center's branches was valued, allowing each site to make its own plans and carry out an initiative according to its own design. "On one hand, you can applaud this because self-motivated centers will not be held back by the corporate process that tends to move more slowly. Conversely, institutionalizing diversity as a business issue will be much harder because of this autonomy," he said.

Some diversity directors reported that the human resources department in their companies was an obstacle. These directors described obstructionist and unsupportive behavior on the part of this department. They found themselves engaged in power struggles and turf battles over the responsibility for implementation of the initiative. "They get in the way, don't follow up on tasks that support the initiative, and sometimes bad mouth the work of the initiative to management. This is a total waste of energy," one director said. Another director reported that her rapport with human resources was civil but that the process was definitely slowed down because the department wanted to be in control. "Human resources thinks that because their domain is people issues, the diversity initiative is a natural fit. It's not."

In small to mid-size organizations, management of a diversity initiative may go directly to human resources as an add-on task. This was reported as an obstacle if there is insufficient people power to get the tasks done and the department does not have the preparation to lead this undertaking.

HUMAN ELEMENTS

Individuals. "Sometimes people intellectually believe they have accepted something, but it still might not sit well with them as a process moves along. For example, in our cultural audit employee groups expressed varying perceptions about what it is like to work for our company. There was a gap in perceptions between white men and males of color, between management and nonmanagement, between factory employees and their supervisors. People resisted what they interpreted as negative feedback," one diversity director reported.

When organizations take a developmental, long-term approach to an initiative and include a needs assessment, there is an inevitable defensiveness by some individuals to the feedback that emerges. In my experience as a consultant, I have heard most directors or CEOs gasp with surprise and anxiety at the results of a needs assessment. For some, it is a shock and disappointment, a dent in the corporate image. This can be a momentary, short-term setback or become an obstacle. If this step is not managed carefully, if clear communication about the meaning and use of the findings is not forthcoming from diversity leadership, an initiative can be derailed. When approaching different phases and tasks in the process of change, diversity directors and organizational leaders can anticipate that there will be both good and bad news. Bad news cannot be avoided, but it can be managed.

An insurance executive I interviewed described different forms of resistance from individuals that became obstacles to his initiative. He labeled them as passive resistance, both conscious and unconscious, and passive/aggressive resistance, also both conscious and unconscious. "It comes in different words and behaviors," he said. "Sometimes it has nothing to do with the initiative. These may be old, unresolved feelings from other organizational frustrations. But some people cannot make the distinction." In psychological terms, these are the defense mechanisms of displacement and projection. A typical example is the employee who goes home and kicks the dog when he would rather kick the boss. For some individuals, the initiative becomes a convenient scapegoat for other workplace issues that have gone unaddressed. Criticism or challenge are outlets to vent anxiety and fear.

Individuals may complain that too much emphasis is being placed on diversity, that funds are diminishing from important programs to go to the initiative, or that it is taking too much time away from regular work. How covert or overt these individuals are with their criticism and resistance is important to notice. I know of incidents, particularly in smaller, less bureaucratic organizations, where employees have taken their complaints about an initiative diversity to a trustee or director, creating an awkward and unpleasant scenario for the agency executive and diversity leader(s).

Human Resources Personnel. Where a diversity director position is not established, managers or directors from human resources are often assigned responsibility for a diversity initiative. One of the operating assumptions is that their specialized focus on people and systems issues predisposes them for the task. This assumption does not apply in all environments I have examined. Where competence in the domain of diversity management is lacking, there is certain to be unnecessary confusion. When commitment to the goals of diversity is not held by individuals charged with this very important work, organizational leaders cannot anticipate the realization of a diversity agenda.

Diversity Director. Another potential obstacle is the diversity director. As I mentioned when discussing enablers, it is essential to have a senior-level person in the role, a person savvy about the forces of organizational culture, respectful of the tedium and slowness of the process, and willing to take cautious risks. A diversity director can become an obstacle to an initiative for a number of reasons. She or he could lack competence to meet the challenges of the role, may be organizationally inexperienced, and may lack support by leadership. I know of a hospital that created a position for a diversity director, hired her, and burned her out in a year. Setting unreasonable expectations that the diversity designee sit on numerous committees, be the clearinghouse for complaints about bias and discrimination, and institute an initiative is a recipe for failure.

Quite often, diversity directors are white women and persons of color, individuals not typically in roles of power in great numbers in any organization. This may make them outsiders and easy marks for criticism because they are different. If they are assigned to the human resources department and not welcomed there, these leaders may experience ostracism and a lack of support. All diversity leaders I spoke with agreed that this is an important role that can be an asset or liability to the process—the organizational conditions have to enable the "best" person for the role.

Consultants. Selection criteria for the use of consultants for different phases and tasks of the diversity initiative have been discussed. I have also heard considerable criticism: "Consultants make promises but don't deliver. They said they can help us with strategic planning but they don't know more than we do. They only stirred up things with their training." It is unfortunate when an organization is disappointed by consultants, because their behavior has a way of adversely impacting the initiative as a whole. When they are perceived as obstacles to the process, diversity planners must reassess their purpose for engaging the consultants and the skill sets necessary to accomplish the task at hand.

Summary

Additional obstacles I have come across fall outside of the categories just discussed. They include finances, external pressures, the impact of education and training, and results. Budgets are a regular part of a discussion of a diversity initiative, and in most organizations it is not a pleasant topic. Most concerns center around how much money will come from other line budgets to go to the initiative, and if there are too few, quick, visible results, judgments about value and expenditures set in. As I demonstrated in Chapter 9 regarding assessing progress and change, there are many ways to demonstrate impact and ongoing, qualitative indicators of return on investment.

Among external pressures that may become obstacles are "noises from the press," as one spokesperson called it. Although multiculturalism and diversity are facts of life, there are still many philosophical challenges expressed through the media that are brought to the workplace. Most diversity leaders reported that they had separated the affirmative action function from that of diversity management, but that this did not eliminate criticisms. "There are unfounded fears about affirmative action and that has an adverse impact on our work. We recognize and deal with it," reported a bank executive.

The impact of education and training is mentioned again because in my experiences the negative consequences of these programs can introduce a long-term problem. I have talked with agency spokespersons who reported that 3 to 5 years after the fact, certain parties still had bad feelings. In other settings, lack of time to process issues that emerged in training or the facilitators' inabilities to manage a discussion led to frustrations that festered and gave bad press to the initiative. The power of these incidents cannot be underestimated, according to leaders who have reported this experience. "It takes a lot of energy and time to redirect the attention to the positive benefits of the initiative."

The last observation picks up again on the topic of results. Too often, the credibility of an initiative is based on visible and measurable results. Keeping activities under wraps too long, specifically more than 6 months, was seen as ill advised by leaders I talked to. "Visible actions are going to bring both positive and negative reactions," said a university director, "but to not communicate will lead to suspicions or misperceptions." Timing is important when it comes to demonstrating results. Although most people want to feel that their concerns are being addressed behaviorally, there may still remain expectations that the initiative will be the cure-all for sexism, workload imbalance, or practices of perceived favoritism. "This is not the real world; some individuals want things to change but do not realize that this is a long-term process. Being on the inside directing the work gives me a real appreciation of the slowness of the process. I cannot let my impatience and that of others become an obstacle," said one diversity director.

Starting Over—Do Differently?

As part of an evaluation process, no less than 2 to 3 years into the process, I like to ask diversity leaders, if you were starting over, what would you do differently? In a few instances, diversity leaders answered that they would not do anything differently. They would go down a similar path, one that reflects their blueprint.

In looking back on their process, other diversity leaders I interviewed pointed to three main things they wished they had done: (a) broaden and empower the base of involvement in the initiative, (b) spend more time with the established advisory councils or committees, and (c) give the initiative more visibility. One bank executive reported that although environmentally "things are more comfortable," to discuss differences, "it would still be preferable not to walk on eggshells," and that through continuous, open discussion this was improving. When speaking of his bank's senior policy council, one executive wished that their diversity planning meetings had been broader, involving others who could bring their perspective. "Having all white men, officers, and senior executives talking to one another about the initiative's progress was a limiting factor. They are least affected by most of the issues mentioned. Sure, they work long, hard hours, but they are well compensated and have the status that a clerk who believes she works just as diligently and loyally will never experience."

Another diversity director reported that he would be certain to get the next level of senior management on board faster. "It's one thing to have the support of the CEO and his direct reports, but it is the next level that needs to be included." The vice president of a manufacturing firm stated that it is important to "address the fears at the senior level, to help them to reframe their thinking about the process. Involve them in building a 3- to 5-year plan. Then they will own it."

Doing more team building for those charged with directing and advising the diversity director was another recommendation made by diversity leaders looking back. "People need to do some self-examination, recognize and move away from impediments. Education about diversity management as a field and the rationale for undertaking it in a given organization is essential. I would definitely add this to the preparation phase," he said.

One strategy recommended for success was to move the process into the infrastructure of the organization and out of the human resources department. Although some organizations had taken this approach, particularly with planning and implementation of strategies, others had not been so inclusive of different parts of the organization from the beginning. Thus, when it came to implementation, they felt restricted by the existing arrangement. Furthermore, these leaders acknowledged, "Real change has to happen throughout all units and people have to want to direct the process themselves." After all, self-determination is a strong U.S. value, one that applies in planning for organizational change.

Guidelines for Identifying Enablers and Pitfalls to Diversity Initiatives

1. Make sure your definition of diversity is inclusive.
2. Create a plan with clear objectives and a focus supported by a business rationale.
3. Realize that one enabler alone cannot support the progress of an initiative; a combination of enablers must be present.
4. Recognize some of the prevalent pitfalls and barriers and try to avoid them.
5. Engage many forces in the organization in the work of the initiative to create a sense of ownership.
6. Anticipate resistance but view it as a natural response to the change process.

7. Be willing to learn from mistakes; they do not have to lead to casualties.
8. Be aware of internal and external factors that affect the initiative.
9. Senior management leadership is essential to an initiative.

11

Modifying Strategic Plans

❑ How can evaluation data inform the initiative?

❑ Will new data cause strategic plans to be modified?

❑ How can we ensure that the plan and initiative will continue to have impact?

❑ Can new strategies for change be introduced at this time?

❑ Decisions to redirect original strategies, to establish new ones, or to eliminate those that have not produced the expected outcome(s) are not unusual in the process of an initiative. Evaluation data typically yield information and other indicators about the progress of outcome-oriented strategies. This, coupled with feedback about the ongoing process garnered outside of the formal evaluation, can also help to inform the continuation of specific plans and tactics, as well as goals for institutionalization of particular policies and practices. Although this may seem a less-complex task than those that occurred previously in the overall diversity management process, responses to the questions raised require deliberate attention in a three-step approach including clarification, reconsideration, and redesign (see Figure 11.1).

In any redesign, diversity leaders should involve individuals familiar with the initiative as it has unfolded as well as some with fresh

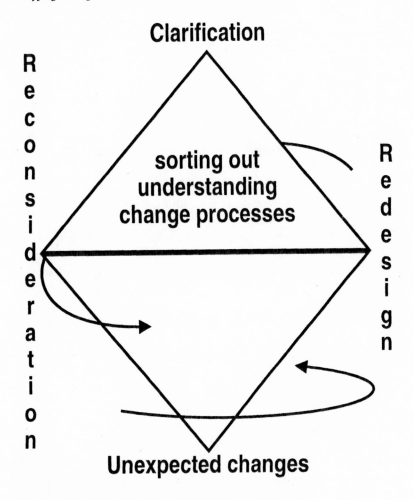

Figure 11.1. Modifying the Strategic Plan
© Empowerment Workshops, Inc.

eyes. Those who know the history of the process are in a better position to compare the needs assessment and the evaluation. As participants in the sorting out of the original findings and the shaping of a plan of action, they also appreciate the rationale for establishing particular goals and strategies and perhaps have some insight about what has and has not worked. "The Diversity Committee really has the pulse of the process. Not only have they influenced everything that has taken place, but they are out on the floor talking with other employees. This helps us to understand why some strategies are moving more slowly. People are tentative about too much change, as they call it, but at least we are hearing this through reliable sources. The modifications to our plan will occur for good reasons," reported an HMO administrator. Conversely, individuals who have not participated on a long-term basis with the initiative may raise questions about particular strategies that others too close to the process have not noticed. Greater objectivity may be introduced by new participants on a committee to balance the potential subjectivity or bias of the others.

Evaluations may take more time and expense, but modifications to the diversity plan equally require formal, intensive attention. I recommend that the three-step process take no more than 6 weeks to complete, although this will vary on the momentum of the initiative in any given organization. Suffice it to say that if it appears that energy and interest is waning, the modification process can give the initiative the boost needed.

Clarification

The question can be asked very simply: Now that we have all of the data from the evaluation, how will we use it? There are several possibilities and procedures. Begin by being clear about what the data indicate. Probe. Question. What does this mean? That the training has not had any impact? That our new mentoring program needs to be offered to other employees, not just women? That including diversity competence on performance evaluations is perceived as punitive?

Be sure that the questions asked and the areas of inquiry in the evaluation have yielded useful data. A well-designed evaluation process should provide data for further planning for the overall initiative. Diversity leaders may not like all of the feedback, but they must view it as helpful to informing new steps.

Another task of clarification is a sorting process. Similar to sorting out the needs assessment, this involves identifying (a) overall highlights of the findings; (b) progress or no progress; (c) change, moving toward change, or no change; (d) institutionalization of what, how, and by whom; and (e) unexpected changes.

SORTING OUT

Findings from the evaluation must be reviewed comprehensively and by goal and strategy. This approach will yield the overall highlights, major findings, and revelations. There may be surprises and disappointments as well. The highlights will likely be progress or change as they relate to the categories of interpersonal behavior, systems, and organizational culture. For example, in one organization, data pointed to increased awareness by the nonmanagement staff of diversity concerns and how the initiative was trying to address them. When new employees joined the agency, they were told the initiative had been a catalyst to addressing issues regarding "groupings" in the lunchroom. According to the diversity director, "It was remarkable because they did this without management involvement. It was informal." The self-interest of different individuals eventually led to increased use of the lunchroom with integrated seating arrangements based on ethnic and racial groupings.

A consumer products firm pointed to increases in sales to women as a result of specially targeted products designed by and for women. Quantifying results and reaching projected sales quotas can reinforce planned strategies. A health care company learned that employee satisfaction increased and that this could be partially attributed to the focus on diversity-related issues. Respondents reported greater interpersonal comfort with coworkers and management as a result of participation on the diversity committee, workshops, and company-wide events that promoted the valuing of all cultural groups. Most individuals were making more of an effort to be respectful in their communication behavior as well, reported an administrator. Overall highlights such as these would seem to indicate that some of the goals and strategies in a strategic plan are being realized and effective.

Determination of progress or no progress can be viewed qualitatively and quantitatively. In one agency, outreach strategies proposed for a new linguistic community were not carried out due to budget cutbacks. This could be viewed as no progress, but the extenuating circumstances should not be overlooked. Because the goal to improve access to this community was still deemed a priority, diversity planners needed to define other means to enable this goal that would not "cost." In this instance, the agency applied for funding from an outside source. Though time-limited, a grant provided the seed funds to move the process along.

One university came to realize that a university-wide coordinator for diversity affairs was not as effective as a person with the same charge within particular departments. This realization, after 3 years, caused school leaders to reconsider the intent and expectations of the coordinator role. Thorough questioning was required. Was the role too ambiguous as feedback suggested? Were the expectations of the individual too grandiose and unreachable? Comparatively speaking, they also had to understand why department coordinators were rated positively. Was their role definition more clear and exacting? Through the questioning process, clarification regarding progress in one area and not in another could be pointed to specifically. This analysis revealed the information sought and allowed university planners to *reconsider* their strategy for a university-wide coordinator. The success of department coordinators also encouraged the establishment of additional posts in other departments, enhancing the original strategy.

UNDERSTANDING CHANGE PROCESSES

Because diversity management initiatives are designed to promote change, assumptions and expectations about change are logical. In the chapter on evaluation, I indicated that questions about change—What is different? What has changed?—will be raised through the formal inquiry process. Change, particularly of a behavioral and measurable nature, is desired. Several human services agencies sought to increase the number of staff with persons of color. To achieve this goal, they employed a number of strategies: Providing internships to graduate students, recruiting on college campuses in the South and Southwest where they had never visited before, and working with recruitment agencies that focused on persons of color. At the time of the evaluation, they were able to report increases in numbers in their talent pool, applications for employment from persons of color, and persons actually hired. With these findings, they could report that the strategies employed were supporting their goal for cultural diversification of staff.

A major corporation set a goal to address work and family issues. The expectations were that the human resources department would establish or change policies to respond to employee concerns, employees would have flexible work hours to accommodate personal needs, and management personnel would be able to respond to employee requests for flextime with consistency and fairness. Inquiries about change included: Were new policies established? What did the new or revised policies provide in response to existing concerns? How were the changes communicated? How did employees experience the changes? In this particular setting, some of the proposed strategies were instituted, but the communication process to support them was lacking. Only a small percentage of employees reported awareness of how the new policy worked, even though the company had distributed brochures throughout the facility. In addition, management practices regarding the policies were still perceived as inconsistent. Further probing became necessary to determine if perception was reality and what kind of additional support managers needed to ensure that all employees understood the policy and were treated fairly when they brought forward their requests regarding work and family issues.

In this latter example, the clarification process was thorough, involving sorting, probing, and analyzing the meaning of the findings. Although tangible change was evident—establishment of a policy, brochures, and requests for flextime by some personnel—the overall impact was negligible. Institutionalization of recommended policies is essential, but without support mechanisms to communicate them effectively and to prepare management personnel to carry them out, work-family and other policies may be just one more item in the company's policy and procedures handbook. For this company and others who had implemented system changes, the important feedback was threefold: (a) the efficacy of the new systems—were they doing what they were designed to do? (b) the nature of implementation—were personnel prepared to communicate with and assist employees? and (c) were employees' needs being met?

Reconsideration and Redesign

The discussion thus far points to an integrated approach to clarify, reconsider, and redesign the diversity plan of action, with clarification getting the most attention. A few comments will be made about the other two elements, as they can further enhance the plan and the initiative as a whole. The feedback from an evaluation causes leaders to pause and reflect on the goals and expectations of the initiative. This process of reconsideration often introduces self-examination: "Rather than giving control of the initiative to one or two people, we realize that if they had left, whatever was gained would have been lost. Internal success should not depend just on a couple of people." Organizations that showed small gains or little impact questioned the seriousness of their efforts. "We weren't giving it enough time," reported one executive. "The good intentions were there, but the work wasn't focused enough."

Other factors of reconsideration are the amount of financial capital budgeted, the visible participation by senior management in the initiative, the visibility of the initiative within the organization, and the capabilities of the diversity director. At the time of the evaluation, organizational leaders learn of employee skepticism about their participation and that of board members. They are also likely to receive an assessment about the diversity director, although this is usually not solicited. Feedback about consultants also invites reconsideration about the selection process for consultants and their capabilities to deliver what is sought.

From clarification and reconsideration comes an opportunity for redesign. As was stated previously, there is a high probability that modifications will be made to most strategic plans. If a thorough plan was developed, the redesign process should be uncomplicated. The redesign task encompasses everything from goals and strategies to the time line and persons responsible for implementation. By continuing to follow the blueprint as it has been customized to apply to the organization, the changes should support the business rationale for diversity management as well as the project outcomes.

Unexpected Changes

Some of the more gratifying feedback from an evaluation is the type that speaks to changes or progress that were not specifically projected. In some of the human services agencies I evaluated, it was revealed that the diversity initiative actually served as the intervention or catalyst to resuscitate floundering organizations. Internal and external forces were squeezing these agencies: Staff was not prepared or available to serve changing client populations, delivery of services was not community based or culturally appropriate, and organizational leadership had limited resources to address increasingly complex issues impacted by funding cutbacks and requirements for stricter documentation.

The introduction of a diversity initiative triggered organizational transformation for more than one agency. By accepting the reality of client and staff diversity and the different needs this presented, organizational leaders, including the board, were able to think proactively about how to seize these seeming obstacles and reframe them as opportunities for the agency. A plan of redesign included creating partnerships with other agencies facing the same issues, including community leaders in the clarification and planning process, and introducing educational seminars to support staff in managing the challenges of change they faced.

I say there was unexpected change because the original diversity-based plan was to recruit personnel to better serve the new cultural and linguistic client population. Because this goal could not be realized without skilled personnel to do the outreach and a budget to compensate the senior-level individuals sought, a number of creative measures were undertaken. Much to the surprise of the board and director, these measures improved the overall recruitment approach for all positions. In addition, staff that had been feeling beleaguered by the situation reported feeling more energized by the fresh focus on something hopeful. Rather than having to think only in terms of cutbacks and doing more with less, they reported increased solidarity among themselves as through seminars they learned more about one another and their hidden strengths that enabled their collective future work. The concept of partnership or teamwork utilized between agencies was applied in the workplace, giving staff members a new way of thinking about their relationship to one another as well as to their clients.

A hospital that was encountering the crunch of managed care, more empty hospital beds, and an increasingly urban versus suburban patient population also experienced multiple positive results from introducing a diversity initiative. Leaders anchored their strategic plan with short- and long-term strategies that allowed them to address the imminent changes more systematically. Earlier, they had provided management training to personnel, but now training was designed to focus on "real" incidents of interpersonal conflict, development of communication skills to attend to new patients, and culture-specific presentations by community leaders. Through the evaluation process, leaders learned about the empowering effects these strategies afforded staff, the improved perception held by neighboring community agencies, and the role modeling the organization provided to other hospitals struggling with the same issues. Another benefit that accrued through this deliberate attention to diversity was leverage with other organizations seeking mergers and with funders inquiring about diversity. The combination of all the strategies also had an impact on the bottom line, because through the development of new and improved specialty services, the hospital was able to fill more beds.

Other examples of unexpected change come through the expansion of the definition of diversity. Where originally the focus was narrow and traditional—on white women and persons of color—the diversity initiative gave voice to other individuals and groups who saw themselves as identifying with the concerns and goals of these two constituencies. A number of organizations became more open to their gay and lesbian employees, enabling them to feel more comfortable and included. Policies and practices in the work and family domain have been modified in several organizations to include gay and lesbian employees as well as individuals in different types of familial relationships.

With other companies, designating business directors and vice presidents with responsibility for diversity-related planning widened the purview of diversity activists to include white men as well. Comparatively speaking, the diversity initiative in these settings took on greater credibility and perceived value because of the involvement of these individuals, usually in positions of power.

My examples point to the likelihood that all organizations can expect some surprises or unexpected impact. In general, this probably speaks to the unpredictability of the change process but also to the idiosyncracies of companies or agencies. What is a surprise in one setting may be commonplace in another.

Summary

The goal of this discussion has been to demonstrate the importance of evaluation data for making adjustments and modifications and designing new directions for the strategic plan of a diversity initiative. In most situations, changes are made to existing strategies rather than to goals of the initiative. Because the vision, goals, and strategic plan are based on a business rationale and findings from the needs assessment, few or minimal modifications should be necessary. Nevertheless, if changes need to be made, it is best that they be done in a timely manner and with a sound rationale. Diversity leaders need to view adjustments as part of the evolutionary process of any change-oriented undertaking. Revisions do not imply failure, poor choices, or bad judgment. Revisions evidence being creative, taking risks, being willing to continue to accept the premise that change is slow and that progress comes in many forms. One coordinator spoke of "trying not to be Type A" about the process, but rather recognize successes and changes on a midyear basis. "If you have set reasonable expectations and goals, you must also learn flexibility and pacing regarding results."

The organizations that experienced unexpected results and learnings were able to support the use of the evaluation process as a tool for further planning. The attention to diversity issues nationally also afforded them a reinforcing message that they were on the right track for organizational development and survival. They came to value the initiative as an enabler to their business strategy and also overcame fears about change that had previously paralyzed them. According to my blueprint, clarification and evaluation are ongoing processes. In this phase, they become even more formalized, provoking many an organization to look forward to them after the first time. Some may view the evaluation as a report card; others see it as an opportunity to improve and modify both effort and performance.

Guidelines for Modifying a Diversity Strategic Plan

1. Use the findings from the evaluation process as a planning tool.
2. The likelihood is that modifications will result from the evaluation process.
3. Before undertaking any modifications, be clear about the meaning of the data.
4. Modify or add strategies to enable goals.
5. Add new goals if this seems necessary but be certain that they support the overall vision and business rationale for the initiative.
6. Think about modifications as additional enablers and new opportunities.
7. Use a three-step process of clarification, reconsideration, and redesign to approach modification of strategic plans.
8. Expect unexpected change.

12

Recognizing and Rewarding Progress

❏ What are indicators of progress?
❏ How can recognition be demonstrated?
❏ Will recognition be an unifying force?

❏ "I would go so far as to say that the greatest of human potentials is the potential of each one of us to empower and acknowledge the other. We all do this throughout our lives, but rarely do we appreciate the power of the empowering we give to others" (Houston, 1982, p. 123). Jean Houston goes on to state that acknowledgment, particularly "during times of confusion" can be an antidote and "stimulus for transformation" (p. 123).

One of the ongoing themes of diversity management initiatives is the need for acknowledgment of progress and change at different levels by different individuals. I have woven this notion into previous chapters to indicate that it is essential to different phases of the initiative and strongly associated with communication strategies that give an initiative visibility, status, and a presence. My belief is that positive reinforcement of events, accomplishments, and individual actions enhance the prestige of the initiative as well as its relationship to ongoing business practices. Because I have addressed this topic previously, the discussion here will be brief and focused on specific activities under-taken by organizations to give recognition, to motivate, and to reward individual contributors. Descriptions will also be made of presenta-tions or award programs at an organizational level, ones that can lift the image of an employer who seriously addresses workforce diversity.

When, What and How

Kick-off events, award dinners, pins, brochures, newsletters, bo-nuses and other incentives, announcements in internal publications, and external media stories—all are examples of the forms and media of recognition and reward in work settings. They may apply to a special issue or cause, such as the United Way; reflect a traditional organizational practice, such as rewarding employees with perfect attendance records; bring attention to a new product, wing of the building, or CEO; or celebrate the organization as a recipient of a local or national award such as the Deming Award for Quality.

Applying similar practices to diversity initiatives, therefore, is not so unusual. Identifying in public ways individual and companywide contributions and accomplishments, the completion of a task very important to the success of an initiative, and the visible demonstration of support of a goal through a planned activity or event are reported by diversity planners.

WHEN

Recognition of progress should occur from the very beginning. In many organizations, the formal announcement of the initiative is heralded as an accomplishment, and the announcement can take vari-ous forms. Some directors talk about an event, usually something social to kick off the process. Several health centers held luncheons with food and music from different cultural groups. The vice president of human resources of a major teaching hospital with a very conserva-tive culture decided to put on a holiday party. As predicted, the event was well attended by all levels of personnel, setting a positive tone for the first meeting of a diversity committee 2 months later. An insurance carrier with an orientation to more formality decided to have a presentation made to all of the senior executives. They in turn were charged to present to their direct reports.

Announcements and events that support the initiative may occur periodically. Several organizations prepare a calendar of events highlighting national and cultural holidays. The calendar is an awareness-building tool as well as a vehicle to keep the diversity initiative present in the daily life of the company. When workforce diversity efforts first began in the late 1980s, many organizations had dedicated months—February was for African Americans, March was for women, September was for Hispanics, and so forth. This practice still continues, putting a continuous focus on diversity.

WHAT AND HOW

The preparation of a diversity mission statement, the appointment of a diversity council, the establishment of an on-site child care facility, and the establishment of a formal mentoring program are all opportunities to be visible and self-affirming.

Columns in company newsletters, updates in an annual report, special posters located throughout offices, and a logo signifying the company's diversity focus are other visible indicators. Many agencies and firms I know of have also developed multilingual materials to profile with target groups. Museums and other cultural institutions have infused multicultural perspectives into exhibits. Others have highlighted the contributions of women, the physically challenged, or immigrants to a particular profession. All of these examples serve to heighten awareness of the breadth of workforce diversity and the many possible ways to infuse it throughout the organization.

Goals to improve community relations or increase workforce diversity often depend on partnership-based strategies. INROADS is a national organization that partners with the private sector to prepare talented college students of color for future work opportunities in the corporate world. Sponsorship of INROADS students has given many companies an opportunity to acknowledge the company's efforts toward workforce diversity and the accomplishment of highly successful interns. Recognition is generally celebrated and formal, including company personnel, interns, alumni, and even parents.

Often, the CEO is invited to participate in an activity to reinforce leadership commitment as well as to acknowledge the work of an individual or group. This appearance is usually deemed significant as well as evidence of the credibility of the initiative.

Other means of recognition are luncheons or awards to contributors. Several organizations I worked with involved a number of employees on diversity task forces for several months. When the task was completed, the entire group was taken to lunch off site and given specially designed pins. Paper weights, pens, and other memorabilia with the company's diversity logo were often awarded. Another organization involved employees in a train-the-trainer program. Throughout their preparation and following the completion of their work, they were acknowledged and rewarded for their contributions above and beyond their normal work functions.

Another method to motivate and reward participants is through the use of performance evaluations. Human resources personnel cited the inclusion of diversity as a performance factor. These formats require employees to meet particular criteria. Based on their performance, reward might result through positive evaluation ratings and even a bonus.

ORGANIZATIONAL FOCUS

Recently, the U.S. Department of Labor instituted the Eve Award. It is designed to motivate organizations to address workforce diversity representation among employees and vendors of government agencies. *Working Woman*, a national magazine, has instituted an evaluation process that results in a listing of top employers for women. These external evaluations serve as incentives to companies who would like to be seen as employers of choice by women. Motivation is thus organizational self-interest and the ability to attract a market of professional women for which there is considerable competition.

Summary

There are many options about how to recognize and reward the progress of a diversity initiative. These are two key themes to the process, essential to support individuals or a particular "happening" that contributes to the greater good of an initiative. I caution diversity leaders to conduct acknowledgments that are appropriate to the spirit of the work at hand. Engaging in only social activities is not the message to send. Celebrating education and training and other endeavors that contribute to systems change may require a different tone and degree of seriousness. Ultimately, recognition and rewards go a long way to promoting the positive benefits of the initiative for the workforce at large.

Guidelines for Recognizing and Rewarding Progress

1. Remember that recognition and rewards must occur throughout the diversity management process.
2. Acknowledgment must manifest in different forms and media.
3. Recognition can occur at an individual and organizational level.
4. Progress can inspire other change efforts in the organization.

13

Developmental Stages of a Diversity Management Process

❑ Are there phases or stages of development?
❑ What are indications of development and change?
❑ Is there a natural process all organizations go through?
❑ How does resistance contribute to development?

One of the basic premises of this book is that there is a blueprint that can guide a change management process catalyzed by diversity. Through my consultation, I have come to recognize the various tasks and milestones that make up this road map, including understanding the domain of diversity management, clarifying motivating factors for an initiative, implementing change-oriented strategies, formally evaluating the process, and modifying strategies based on an evaluation of the initiative. For each phase in the blueprint, I have also proposed a framework that includes planning and design; implementation through a deliberate set of procedures and strategies; and ongoing clarification, evaluation, and recognition of progress. A review of the diversity management process in a variety of organizations—each with its own unique business culture—has also shown me that there are *developmental stages* that can be attributed to a deliberate change initiative.

In this chapter, I outline the following developmental stages: exploration, commitment, experimentation, redefinition, consolidation or integration, and regeneration (see Figure 13.1). How do these differ from the phases in my blueprint? They do not actually differ, rather, they introduce a complementary perspective to the tasks and functions that are more readily observable. Developmental stages are dynamic and evolutionary and usually sequential. With diversity management initiatives, designed to impact organizational culture, interpersonal behavior, and systems, changes in thinking, emotions, and behavior can be anticipated. In Chapter 1, I discussed the mind-set necessary to establish diversity initiatives. Throughout the subsequent chapters, I described different behaviors that enable diversity management processes to become operationalized. As I discuss stages of organizational change, I believe it is also essential to give attention to the range of emotions that often manifest during a diversity management initiative. Here, I focus particularly on resistance and negative reactions to the change process.

At this juncture, I would like to note that the topic of diversity continues to provoke strong political and sociocultural reactions. The reporting of these reactions through public forums and, particularly, through media hyperbole has raised the level of awareness among people in general, but simultaneously provoked wide-ranging emotions among many employees. Many groups and individuals have a predetermined mind-set about diversity, one that is not favorable, but becomes introduced into the organizational change process. In most settings, I have observed that it is a more resistant mind-set. Although psychologically resistance is a form of change, I also recognize that for organizational and diversity leaders, understanding potential emotional reactions to the introduction and development of a diversity management initiative is essential.

The Developmental Stages

The introduction of a diversity management initiative, as has been discussed, precipitates questioning about rationale, need, and direction. Why are we doing this? What are we going to gain from it? What will change and how will this affect me? Questions at a personal level

Figure 13.1. Organizational Development Through Diversity Management
© Empowerment Workshops, Inc.

always occur and vary from business-motivated questions. How will this benefit the organization—people, productivity, and profits? How much will it cost? The connection between diversity management and business planning was described in Chapter 1. In my discussion, I stated that an initiative can be viewed as (a) a strategic organizational approach, (b) a bridge between human diversity and business goals and practices, (c) a proactive rather that reactive approach to emerging markets, and (d) a catalyst to promote individual and organizational change. These premises, I believe, orient an initiative to the proposed developmental stages of exploration, commitment, experimentation, redefinition, consolidation or integration, and regeneration. Although they are described as sequential, these stages may recur during more than one phase of the blueprint and may also occur simultaneously.

STAGE ONE: EXPLORATION

Leaders at an urban university realized that decreased enrollment would continue due to increasing competition, high costs, and the lack of a large population of entry-level students in the United States. This awareness motivated them to explore avenues to remain viable and increase their "market share" of the college population. This involved gathering data that included demographic projections for traditional college students (18- to 22-year-olds), emerging markets including working adults and foreign markets, and approaches taken by other universities. Staff also initiated discussions with local organizations, schools, and community groups about collaborative undertakings. Their findings strongly suggested that future planning would require inclusion of more nontraditional, non-American student populations; creating partnerships with nonacademic institutions that would support the expanding mission of the university; and delivering education through more technologically advanced formats. The message university leaders gathered through exploration was that they had to do their business differently in several areas: marketing and recruitment of new students, community relations, information systems, and advertising.

The stage of exploration serves to confirm, inform, and otherwise clarify the status quo of a business or organization. Often, the findings from an exploratory process create alarm, surprise, or simply an opportunity to begin new change. The tasks the university engaged in correspond to two phases of the blueprint: clarifying motivators and data gathering.

STAGE TWO: COMMITMENT

The same university leaders and planners, cognizant of the literature about diversity management as a new business domain, decided to establish a diversity initiative to support their broad, organizational process of change. They made a formal commitment to the initiative by establishing a council, appointing a vice president, and integrating specific strategies into the university master plan. In addition, they wrote vision and mission statements regarding diversity that became public documents at the university. These tasks coincide with the blueprint's vision and goal-setting phase.

Examples of commitment at one insurance company included a kickoff ceremony and a companywide communication to formally announce the establishment of the initiative. At a bank with multiple branches, internal and external publications carried statements from chief officers about the initiative as well as pictorial examples of diversity strategies in action, that is, senior citizens and families of color transacting business. Other organizations I have worked with exhibited their commitment through the appointment of a diversity vice president or director. Each of these examples involved dedicated financial and human resources, essential enablers to the success of an initiative.

STAGE THREE: EXPERIMENTATION

The introduction of any new change-driven effort can be at best termed experimental. Although compelling research and development may indicate that a new product will be successful, there are examples to the contrary. Perhaps one of the best known is the Chevy Nova automobile. In spite of well-grounded plans, the car did not sell in Latin American countries. Much to the chagrin of the manufacturer, the term *nova* in Spanish (*no va*) means "no go." This was a costly experiment.

A holistic approach to diversity management means addressing organizational culture, interpersonal behavior, and systems, a complex undertaking. As organizational planners have learned, this multidimensional framework requires engagement of many individuals and innovative strategies to address goals and objectives. Although an entire initiative can be termed experimental, in this discussion I point to the prioritization and implementation of strategies phase of the blueprint as more specific to the application of this developmental stage.

The creation of a strategic plan signals the initiation of new and continuing activities and processes: constituting committees, planning education and training programs, partnering with other organizations, creating diversity action plans by business units, reviewing existing policies and practices, rewriting mission statements and bylaws, developing public relations materials, and engaging in different types of marketing and communications are among the array of enabling factors that support an initiative. Theoretically and practically, they are formulated and implemented to respond to existing concerns and issues. Although they may be anchored in business-oriented goals and may have been successful for other initiatives, there is no guarantee that they will all bring the desired results.

Many organizations use pilot programs to try out some of their change-related strategies. The vice president of one hospital reported that her initial 2-year plan was designed to ease in the diversity initiative. The response to introductory efforts, including a hospital-wide holiday gathering, gave her a green light to continue more aggressively over the next 3 to 5 years.

In my experience, thinking about strategies—particularly early strategies—as experiments can reduce the pressure on expected outcomes and allow room to say: "Let's try it," or "It didn't work; we may not have been ready for that," or "Next time, we will communicate differently about our plans." In most organizations, I have found that a diversity initiative is so highly scrutinized that it behooves diversity directors and planners to assume a certain experimental approach to initiatives, and given this, to stay open to feedback. To ignore feedback may undermine the initiative's future. In spite of a mind-set based on commitment and well-grounded plans of action, there needs to be a recognition that with any change-oriented initiative, success comes in different forms and times, and not always as predicted.

STAGE FOUR: REDEFINITION

The process of redefinition can be identified during several phases of the blueprint: during the data analysis, during goal and strategy planning, and following the formal evaluation. Redefinition can focus on the purview of the diversity initiative (perhaps it was too ambitious?). At times, redefinition could apply to particular goals or the focus of specific efforts, for example, retention of women professionals, work reassignment, or the language and medium used to describe the initiative. Most redefinitions occur following formal evaluation(s).

A manufacturing company learned following two sessions of management training that employees resented the lack of earlier participation by senior management. Diversity planners listened to the feedback and redesigned the training schedule so that senior personnel would attend earlier.

When mergers and other complex reorganizations occur, diversity directors have to pause and assess the status and direction of their initiative. One hospital had a strong initiative under way at the time of their merger. The partner institution had no like initiative under way. Although the first hospital continued to implement its goals and strategies, planners acknowledged that it would be necessary to do some redefinition with their new partner. After 2 years of a formal diversity initiative with appointed leaders representing staff and management, a human services agency decided to assign responsibility for all of its diversity-related plans to the agency's executive management team. For this agency, redefinition meant making the initiative an integral part of business planning, not separate from the mainstream.

STAGE FIVE: CONSOLIDATION OR INTEGRATION

The last example I used above also serves to exemplify the stage of consolidation or integration. Often, this stage results in diversity-related goals and strategies becoming part of organizational operations. Rather than continuing with specific diversity management training, an organization could fold elements of the program into existing, companywide training that all managers must attend. Leaders in one organization I talked to redesigned their annual report to highlight outcomes of diversity efforts; previously a special diversity report had been published. A professional association developed guidelines for its continuing education offerings: Presenters were now required to comment on the relevance or limitation of their presentation for generalization to culturally diverse individuals.

These are all examples of integration of new perspectives into existing systems and practices leading to institutionalization. A strategy or activity that was once targeted to support a diversity-based goal becomes absorbed into mainstream policies and practices. It no longer stands alone. Funders of the 50 diversity initiatives I evaluated believe that institutionalization is an indicator of success. When a policy or practice becomes part of the organizational culture's way of doing business, real impact can be cited, they believe. Behavioral outcomes are key indicators of change and growth.

STAGE SIX: REGENERATION

Regeneration indicates renewal, reformation, and reestablishment. As might be expected, continuous changes nationally and globally—political, technological, social, and environmental—are factors that impact organizations. These may require bringing into existence again the principles and vision of diversity management initiatives.

When new challenges to an initiative appear, an opportunity to invoke and restate the thinking and strategies initially utilized with the initiative may be called for.

At the time of implementation of specific strategies designed to support a diversity initiative, I have encouraged diversity planners to restate the rationale for the focus on diversity. Because the rationale is grounded in organizational goals, it helps to explain and reassure participants about purpose and intent. Communication, even over-communication, must continue.

A Psychological Perspective on the Diversity Change Process

> For many people change is frightening, it moves us out of our comfort zone. We knew how to interact and be successful in the old culture. But it is very scary when the rules change. At the same time that we say we want change, we will also resist. (Katz, 1992, p. 1)

There are psychological processes that I believe accompany each of the developmental stages just described. Very simply, they include cognitive, affective, and behavioral processes working together—sometimes consciously, other times unconsciously. For each stage of development, an organization engages in a cognitive process that includes elements of recognition, identification, analysis, questioning, and clarification. This reflects a more objective, logical, intellectual, and at times academic approach and is a critical component to diversity initiatives because it can help to explain the philosophy and rationale for the use of a particular framework to facilitate the process. Leaders in some organizations contend that theirs is an entirely pragmatic perspective—for business reasons. But from purely psychological constructs, this is not really possible, as all change initiatives—particularly ones that focus on diversity—provoke a range of emotional responses. Festinger (1957) called this *cognitive dissonance*, referring to an internal reaction when our perceived reality and predictability is destablized.

When an organization's sense of sameness and predictability is challenged, several types of responses arise based on individuals' perception of the organizational culture. For those who think that everything is fine just as it is, there is an assumption that promoting change is unnecessary. I have found that this is particularly true for profitable companies. "If we are so successful, why poke around?" "Employees like working here. It's like one happy family." "We're diverse already. There are several women and gays in management." Other individuals may accept these statements but also have another perspective based on work and real-life experiences. They may be individuals who feel marginalized, not part of "in" groups or in power roles, or with issues not historically addressed in the workplace. "It's about time we looked openly at the sexual harassment that occurs, but it just does not feel safe to talk with managers about this." "You have to have a sponsor to fit in or know what lies ahead." It is usually through cultural audits that I hear both types of reaction. From the same employee who supports an initiative may come cynical comments: "We talked to some other consultants 10 years ago, nothing changed." Some staff may experience renewed feelings of frustration, whereas others who think everything is "fine" may be annoyed about the focus on diversity or react with indifference.

Resistance and support can be both verbal and nonverbal. Some individuals may actively express relief that something is being done to address diversity as a business issue; others may challenge or question the merits of the process. Critics may come from any place in the organization, but I have often found middle managers to be the most frustrated. Middle managers are often delegated new tasks when a diversity initiative begins, and feedback from needs assessments often points to management personnel as "problems." Understandably, they may resent and perhaps resist the assignments involving their participation. Some examples were cited in earlier chapters: individual managers struggling with human resources personnel or the diversity director about their responsibility to the initiative or with consultants about how to deliver a training program. When individuals experience a loss of control, they are likely to react, not respond.

In my experience, all organizations go through some emotional highs and lows as they undergo a diversity initiative. Steps of an initiative that can be expected to make emotional waves include the initiative's commencement, when findings from the needs assessment are revealed, at the onset or involvement of more individuals in strategy planning and implementation, the beginning of training, when accountability through performance evaluations or other measures is introduced, and at the time of a formal evaluation.

Instances of Dissonance

Dissonance is common when diversity management is introduced. Fixed thinking may be challenged; anxieties, fears, and excitement may be provoked; and surprising behavior may result, sometimes from those who are perceived as levelheaded, liberal, or aloof. Organizational culture may appear to hold constant, but individuals experiencing some form of interruption to their life order at work will try to avoid the short- and long-term effects of a change process. "People felt put upon. They did not see why we had to change the artwork in the waiting room and put in multilingual literature. Some actually thought it was patronizing. Thank goodness for those who saw the value of the change. Their enthusiasm helped to offset the criticism," said a diversity director. "Beginning the diversity initiative was the shot in the arm this place needed. We were going along, getting things done, but morale was flat, staff satisfaction was down, and patient complaints were up. Organizationally, it holds a lot of promise but people don't like change, especially if they can't relate to it. That's changing. Now more people see how our goals include them too."

Resistance to Change

In an earlier chapter, I made reference to the use of defense mechanisms, or unconscious reactions based on fears, anxiety, or other unresolved emotions. I offer a brief description of some of these defenses in the context of the diversity management process. Denial is a defense mechanism I often see when an initiative is introduced. "If we don't talk about it, it will go away," seems to be the inner thought of a denier. "We don't have a problem here. Everyone gets along, is treated fairly. We don't discriminate."

Displacement is another defense mechanism. This could affect any work relationship, but I use the example here of a manager and subordinate. A manager, upset that he has to release his employees to attend a mandatory training or that he has to go himself, may take it out on those he supervises by barking orders, finding faults unnecessarily, and so on. Rather than voicing his complaint to the appropriate parties, he misdirects it to an innocent victim.

Projection, another defense mechanism, occurs when the same manager says something like, "We're handling everything just fine here. We have always dealt with diversity issues." Or, "I'm not racist. I have plenty of black friends. It's really senior management who should be sitting here discussing these issues. We hope you talk to them too." Individuals who project do not take responsibility for their behavior. Instead, they project their own problem and behavior onto others, proclaiming themselves innocent.

Blame is another classic defense. "It's those women and minorities who are always complaining." "If this country weren't so generous, we would stop the invasion of foreigners." This defense creates a way of escaping responsibility. "Senior management wants us to take the heat. This is all their fault for bad decisions they made, and they get a much better salary too."

The last defense mechanism I shall mention is intellectualization. Individuals using this defense may use arguments based on statistics, on legislation established on behalf of particular groups, or on U.S. history to support their reservations. "Our figures indicate that our workforce is 30% persons of color. They're not in management yet, but in the future . . ." or "Affirmative action does not work for us because we have 'too many' women already." When leading training, I have heard criticism of the limitations of a self-assessment because it was not scientific or that data reported are too old and not relevant to the given setting.

The bottom line is that resistance, in its many forms, is part of a diversity management initiative, and it occurs in all types of organizations and industries. I have many examples to cite. Resistance may involve employees refusing to attend a focus group or interview or challenging coworkers who sit on councils or advisory boards. It could involve acting out during training sessions, avoiding events that focus on the initiative, or bad-mouthing the initiative or its leaders.

My point in focusing on the emotions that can arise during a change process and their manifestations is to make it clear that they are normal reactions to a diversity initiative. I do not mean to condone some of the more hostile and disrespectful reactions that can occur, but I suggest that such responses be anticipated. For organizational leaders and diversity directors, resistance should be expected, not come as a surprise.

Summary

What does all of this say about organizational change through diversity management? That exploration, affirmation or commitment, experimentation, redefinition, consolidation or integration, and regeneration are natural stages on the way to becoming a multicultural organization. Each of these stages brings along with it dynamics of change and thought-provoking challenges that in turn impact emotions and behavior. These are unavoidable. Diversity leaders and consultants agree that these developmental stages are evident retrospectively. With the 50 diversity initiatives I examined, funders and planners were able to identify these discrete stages as well as an increase in the level of activity as the initiatives continued. In other words, momentum increases as the process moves forward, inspiring a sense of optimism as well as demonstrating examples of integration.

14

The Future of
Diversity Management

- ❑ Will diversity continue to be a business issue?
- ❑ Will the focus on diversity management expand or wane?
- ❑ What are the current learnings that can contribute to future initiatives?
- ❑ What are the best practices?

As we move into a new century, what is the future of diversity as a business issue? The unanimous response of those who are informed about this question is that the focus on diversity in the workplace is here to stay. What's more, many predict that diversity management will expand into new settings. "Continued success relies on employing talented people. In the context of the world community, people are very different. Employing culturally sound practices that surround these human and cultural differences is essential," reported a diversity vice president.

Generally speaking, thinking and planning for the future of a diversity initiative requires reflection on several factors: original and current motivators for engaging in diversity management, findings from the evaluation, and the organization's long-term business plan.

Discussions with organizational leaders and planners have revealed both *internal* and *external* criteria that support the need to continue a diversity management focus. Among the external factors frequently cited are emerging markets, international migrations, technological advancements, the requirement of new skill sets (linguistic, cultural, technical, management, etc.), and the increasing population of persons of color in the United States. Internal forces include organizational restructuring, increased cultural and linguistic diversity in the workplace, more white women and persons of color in professional and managerial roles, the need for effective interpersonal communication, competition for talent, practices that motivate and reward a diverse workforce, self-interest, and continued business success.

What is often clear after an organization has engaged in diversity management efforts is that the motivation for continuing this focus grows. Progress and factors of success become reinforcing agents, catalysts, and harbingers of additional future opportunities. Successful outcomes based on planned goals are compelling, leading to a renewed commitment to an initiative and integration of new management practices into the mainstream business culture. Together, these contribute to an even stronger business case for diversity.

Emerging and Future Markets

"We define diversity as part of the way we do business—focus on emerging markets and their purchasing power," reported a bank executive. "When we establish a branch in a particular location, we need to understand the people who reside in that community. We use micromarketing as a management tool." Among the strategies this bank used to reach potential Vietnamese and Russian immigrant customers were highlighting individuals from those groups in advertisements, spelling out their effect on the business of the whole institution, creating bilingual communications that were more than simplistic translations, staffing branch offices with representative personnel, and providing staff development for more-effective intercultural communication and customer relations.

Discussions with representatives of the same bank underscored that motivation to change the institutional infrastructure was driven both by potential new business and domestic and global competition. "We need to change because of foreign interests in banking. The largest banks in the world are not in the United States. We may have only one on the top 10 list, yet business trends are global." Comments about personnel preparedness, particularly based on cultural behavioral practices from country to country, were cited as critical to success in this new market. "We cannot impose our way of doing business. Interpersonal relationship building is key in other cultures." A working knowledge of cross-cultural differences was mentioned by all of those interviewed. Through firsthand experience, they could identify the benefits of culturally informed and respectful practices. "It can be as simple as how you greet someone," or in the case of a hospital, having receptionists who are bilingual. Appearances, voices, words, and other indications of respectful behavior are increasing in importance.

Other market shifts are influenced by the retirement and new baby-boomer populations. A diversity director discussed how individuals representing different age, cultural, gender, and socioeconomic groups have been socialized to perceive banks. For example, most of today's senior citizens prefer to walk into the bank for their transactions and expect to be known personally by a teller or customer services agent. On the other hand, college students may relate primarily to automatic teller machines out of convenience and familiarity.

A colleague at a financial agency related an example about an insurance agent from California. One of his salespersons decided to pursue the business of migrant workers, individuals for whom it was difficult to impossible to seek such services. In spite of perceptions about this group's economic limitations, he decided to go into their territory. What resulted was success in this niche market. Foremost in this successful endeavor was the focus on interpersonal relationships. He had to build trust and credibility through equally legitimate representatives of the workers. It was a slow process that led to positive outcomes for many—the clients, the salesperson, and the company.

I have spoken to many diversity directors charged with supporting human resources departments by searching for talent to increase representation. They spoke emphatically about the need to create an environment that is inclusive and in which differences are respected. "If persons of color are perceived only as affirmative action hires, not individuals hired for their skill sets, we are never going to be able to have the diverse workforce we talk about. Insiders, not just the new-comers need to be adaptable," one director said. Diversity directors also spoke about the need to recognize how organizational norms and practices may be perceived by underrepresented individuals. "If you are constantly given a message that you do not fit, why would you stay?"

Products

With an eye toward current and future markets, business leaders are recognizing that new products should be developed with particular clientele in mind. It is reported that the disposable income of persons of color in the United States is $600 billion. Turning again to the banking industry, attention to small business owners—particularly women and immigrants—is becoming more focused. Historically, women have not been seen as primary consumers by many businesses, but clearly this has changed over the past 20 years as their presence in the workplace and small business markets has grown. For a bank representative, attention may mean not assuming what the potential customer does or does not know about banking products. Women who are treated with condescending or patronizing behavior are likely to take their business elsewhere. Furthermore, women who establish small businesses are consumers who present wide-ranging interests and backgrounds. Not only individualized service is required but also an approach devoid of stereotypical assumptions about women. An international consumer products company addressed both gender and cultural differences in its growth strategy. For the development of female-oriented products, women researchers and designers were involved. To market these same products globally, an investigation of cultural norms to determine the potential receptiveness to these items was undertaken.

Similar considerations have been described to me in relation to shifting immigrant populations. As new waves of refugees and immigrants reach the United States, there are new clients to consider. Among the newcomers to the New England area are Central Americans, Haitians, Eastern Europeans, and Russians. Similar settlement patterns (although the countries of origins may be different) are being seen in other regions of the country. To return to the banking example, although some of theses newcomers may be inexperienced with U.S. banking procedures, this does not necessarily mean that they did not use banks in their home country. Conversely, some of these immigrants may not have used banks because they perceived them as government agencies and therefore untrustworthy. Marketing to new groups requires both technical and cultural competence. The more knowledge about cultural norms and practices of these immigrant groups a business has, the greater likelihood successful exchanges will result.

Another industry we can turn to for examples of working with the immigrant customer is real estate. Immigrants, particularly in urban areas where they settle, are seen as potential homeowners by this industry, and having agents who speak their language or are bicultural themselves is seen as leverage. In an interview, a naturalized U.S. citizen from China reported that until he worked with a Chinese American agent he had not experienced a sense of being understood. Although he had had sufficient money to buy a new home for more than 10 years, he did not make the purchase until he worked with this agent. International migrations are likely to continue as long as the United States is seen as a desirable destination, and bilingual ability and cultural competence on the part of personnel will become valuable assets in this changing marketplace.

The other side of emerging markets is the tendency of American-owned companies to open subsidiaries outside of the United States. Although this has been done for many years, current research shows that the numbers of international customers and the need to send U.S. workers abroad seems to be increasing. "Growth areas are outside of the United States. We are motivated by worldwide issues that come home, so we need to examine these carefully if we want the greatest market share," stated the vice president for diversity of a global manufacturing firm. The preparation of employees for overseas assignments is perceived as essential to their performance in the context of their function as well as their being cultural brokers. Being bilingual and possessing cultural knowledge for an assignment are deemed more highly desirable. Today, regardless of the industry—advertising, health care, financial services, manufacturing, high tech, education, or human services—attention to emerging markets is a top priority. My conversations with business leaders have highlighted this need as a diversity business issue again and again.

Self-Interest

"In the context of diversity as we have defined it—*it is about all people and all of our issues*—it is important for our company; it is in our self-interest. Our workforce is 80% demographically diverse [non-white, non-European]. Continued success relies on employing talented people and having employment practices that surround these human and cultural differences," one diversity director said. A human resources director described her organization's interest in diversity succinctly: "Diversity needs to be a functional part of our business to be effective globally." The director of a cultural institution asserted that for continued success and relevance to changing domestic markets, "Diversity would become part of the fabric" of the institution's business plans.

Interviewers who spoke of self-interest have done so based on *reality* rather than abstract thinking about diversity as a potentially self-serving commodity. Organizations in the delivery of human services recognize the squeeze from funding cuts, managed care increase in operating costs, and decreases in their endowment funds. "We are competing with other social services agencies for clients, corporate sponsorship, funding, and educational partnerships. Diversity is on everyone's checklist. We have to demonstrate how we are currently addressing diversity and a vision statement is not enough," asserted an agency director.

Technological Advancement

In my experience, technology has often been identified as a force that relates directly to human diversity as the human resources departments and leaders of these industries reconsider their expectations in terms of education, accessibility, and skill sets. Age, cultural, educational, gender, and linguistic differences among workers are critical considerations when technology is a business driving force. "It requires adaptability, preparedness, and long-term planning. If you know that literacy is going to be essential to operate new machinery, what does that mean for the current workforce who speaks English as a second language or English-speaking employees who never had to use reading skills to complete a task?" This director of manufacturing also observed that although women's access to engineering and other technical training prepared them for many jobs, gender bias by both men and women continued to be a barrier to their advancement. "They have the skills, but the organizational culture has not been very adaptable. We have lost a number of good women as a result."

Focusing on technology also tends to introduce discussions about the perceptions of Asians as good technical but not managerial workers. Just as the hard sciences have always been seen as a male field, so too has this type of thinking been generalized to Asian cultural groups. This mind-set often leads to pigeonholing or unrealistic expectations of Asian men and women based on stereotypes. It is also appropriate to state that the stereotypes that exist for all individuals and groups relative to work ability create expectations both positive and negative that can help some individuals while prejudicing others.

Advancements in technology often spell more global business opportunities. As has been widely acknowledged, "work becomes complicated by communication styles, patterns, and language ability," indicated a high-tech executive. She also noted that many of the countries where business is expanding happen to be populated by persons of color, often individuals who reflect the major ethnic and racial minority groups in the United States. "The technological age requires skills that need to be accessible to persons of color in the United States. They may be the most appropriate cultural and business brokers in other parts of the world."

Increased Human Differences in the Workplace

Being in a knowledge age will continue to drive concerns about worker preparedness as well as the future worker. Increased partnerships between public schools and business are preventive measures to ensure that current students, particularly in urban settings, are prepared with the technical knowledge and skills to compete in the future.

Johnston and Packer's (1987) *Workforce 2000* projections speak of trends portending the increase of white women, immigrants, and people of color in the workplace. Many organizations realize that diversity is not only about numerical representation but about relationships, management practices, and a workplace culture that respects human differences as assets and not problems that may go away. The recent focus on workforce diversity has drawn attention to the worker, customer, board member, and executive in a more exact and complex manner than has ever been done before. Issues of supply and demand will always exist, but attention to human differences has gone beyond race and gender. Other individuals in the workforce are asking for consideration as well: the physically challenged, gays and lesbians, older workers, parents, and others are raising their voices. Through cultural audits, business leaders have learned that not all employees feel valued and respected and that this in turn can impact job performance and productivity. It has always been acknowledged that different individuals require different forms of motivation, incentives, and rewards. A combination of factors such as increasing global business markets, downsizing, higher numbers of aging workers, and changing business markets have caused the focus on personnel to become more intentional. Through market research, businesses are paying more attention to the spending patterns of women and ethnic-specific consumers, for example. These changes support one of the fundamental premises of diversity management asserted in Chapter 1, that it promotes the connection between people and business goals.

Summary

Attention to workforce diversity has fostered and supported attention to integrated business strategies including leadership, total quality, continuous learning, communication, and multicultural competence. Companies are increasingly recognizing that success through diversity depends on individual and organizational empowerment, shared commitment, and a willingness to change.

Continuous learning is one key to diversity management, and organizations are realizing that training in the name of diversity must be strategic and linked to business practices that will lead to increased performance and respectful interpersonal relationships. My empowerment philosophy states that all people are capable of new learning and change provided they have a context that facilitates and recognizes this progress. Creativity in the workplace is immense, but often untapped.

Companies that assess their rationale for diversity management may come to agree with one of my premises: that organizations and people are in interdependent relationships. Employees can be their most valued resource provided they are viewed this way.

Best Practices

The field of diversity management continues to evolve, and as organizational leaders report, it has a broad future as long as human differences intersect with business goals. Organizations that have benefited through their focus on diversity management have shared with me a rich set of experiences that I have related in this book. These organizations have a collective legacy to pass on to others who have not approached change through diversity. As a way of summarizing their learnings and recommendations, I reiterate the following guidelines of best practices:

1. Develop a business rationale for diversity.
2. Educate senior managers so that they can develop and support the business rationale.
3. Customize your diversity management approach so that it will not create culture shock but rather is respectful of the organizational cultural norms.
4. Commitment should come in the form of leadership, participation of a representative workforce, and dedicated human and financial resources.
5. Individuals charged with responsibility for diversity management must be knowledgeable, credible, and well-grounded personally and professionally.
6. Building knowledge through audits, benchmarking, and other sources is essential to the development of a relevant strategic plan.
7. Diversity-driven goals and strategies can be centralized or driven through business units and departments.
8. All strategies should be evaluated intermittently.
9. Training and education must be linked to business goals and practices.

10. Some type of formal evaluation to measure impact and institution-alization should take place at the end of the second year of an initiative.
11. Modification of strategic goals and strategies is inevitable.
12. Changes must be made in systems, policies, and procedures that impact the workforce.
13. Organizational change through diversity to meet desirable business goals can be systematically planned and implemented.
14. Visibility must be given to the initiative within and outside of the organization to reinforce credibility.

References

Adler, N. J. (1986). *International dimensions of organizational behavior.* Boston: PWS-Kent.

Americans With Disabilities Act of 1990, 42 U.S.C.A. § 12101 *et seq.* (West 1993).

Arredondo, P., & Glauner, T. (1992). *Personal dimensions of identity model.* Boston: Empowerment Workshops.

Arredondo, P., Toporek, R., Brown, S., Jones, J., Locke, D. C., Sanchez, J., & Stadler, H. (1996). Operationalizing the multicultural counseling competencies. *Journal of Multicultural Counseling and Development, 24,* 42-78.

Beer, M., Eistenstat, A., & Spector, B. (1990). *The critical path to corporate renewal.* Boston: Business School Press.

Chemers, M., Oskamp, S., & Costanzo, M. A. (1995). *Diversity in organizations.* Thousand Oaks, CA: Sage.

Civil Rights Act of 1964, as amended, 42 U.S.C. § 2000E *et seq.* (1964).

Cox, T. H., Jr. (1993). *Cultural diversity in organizations.* San Francisco: Berrett-Koehler.

De Pree, M. (1992). *Leadership jazz.* New York: Currency Doubleday.

Drucker, P. F. (1992). *Managing for the future.* New York: Truman Talley Books/Plume.

Drucker, P. F. (1993). *Post capitalist society.* New York: HarperCollins.

Festinger, L. (1957). *A theory of cognitive dissonance.* Stanford, CA: Stanford University Press.

Gould, S. J. (1994, November). The geometer of race. *Discover,* pp. 65-69.

Handlin, O. (1941). *Boston's immigrants: A study in acculturation.* Boston: Little, Brown.

Hannerz, U. (1992). *Cultural complexity.* New York: Columbia University Press.

Harris, P. R., & Moran, R. T. (1979). *Managing cultural differences.* Houston, TX: Gulf Publishing.

Houston, J. (1982). *The possible human.* Los Angeles, CA: J. P. Tarcher, Inc.

Johnston, W. B., & Packer, A. H. (1987). *Workforce 2000: Work and workers for the twenty-first century.* Indianapolis, IN: Hudson Institute.

Kanter, R. (1995). *World class.* New York: Simon & Schuster.

Kohls, R. (1984). *Values Americans live by.* Washington, DC: Meridian House International.

Kroeber, A. L., & Kluckhohn, C. (1952). *Culture: A critical review of concepts and definitions.* New York: Vintage.

Katz, J. (1992). Resistance is part of the change process. *Cultural Diversity at Work, 5*(1), 1-10.

Larkin, T. J., & Larkin, S. (1994). *Communicating change.* New York: McGraw-Hill.

Lawrence, P. R. (1969). How to deal with resistance to change. *Harvard Business Review, 47,* 77-85.

Locke, D. C. (1992). *Increasing multicultural understanding.* Newbury Park, CA: Sage.

Loden, M., & Rosener, J. B. (1991). *Workforce America.* Homewood, IL: Business One Irwin.

Morrison, A., Ruderman, M. N., & Hughes-James, M. (1993). *Making diversity happen.* Greensboro, NC: Center for Creative Leadership.

Naisbett, J., & Aburdene, P. (1985). *Reinventing the corporation.* New York: Warner.

Nanus, B. (1992). *Visionary leadership: Creating a compelling sense of direction for your organization.* San Francisco: Jossey-Bass.

Peters, T. (1987). *Thriving on chaos.* New York: Harper & Row.

Peters, T. (1992). *Liberation management.* New York: Fawcett Columbine.

Reingold, E. (1990, January 22). Facing the "totally new and dynamic." *Time,* pp. 6-7.

Schneider, B. (1987). The people make the place. *Personal Psychology, 40,* 437-453.

Schultz, S. K. (1973). *The cultural factory: Boston public schools, 1789-1860.* New York: Oxford University Press.

Simons, G. F., Vazquez, C., & Harris, P. R. (1993). *Transcultural leadership: Empowering the diverse workforce.* Houston, TX: Gulf Publishing.

Simpson, J. B. (1988). *Simpson's contemporary quotations.* Boston: Houghton Mifflin.

Smith, T. (1993). *Parzival's briefcase.* San Francisco: Chronicle Books.

Spence, J. (1985). Achievement American style. *American Psychologist, 40*(12), 1285-1295.

Stewart, E. (1972). *American cultural patterns: A cross-cultural perspective.* Pittsburgh: University of Pittsburgh, Intercultural Communication Network.

Sue, D. W. (1995). Multicultural organizational development. In J. Ponterotto, J. M. Casas, L. A. Suzuki, & M. Alexander (Eds.), *Handbook of multicultural counseling* (pp. 474-492). Thousand Oaks, CA: Sage.

Sue, D. W., Arredondo, P., & McDavis, R. J. (1992). Multicultural competencies and standards: A call to the profession. *Journal of Counseling & Development, 20,* 64-88.

Sue, D. W., & Sue, D. (1990). *Counseling the culturally different* (2nd ed.). New York: John Wiley.

Thomas, R. R., Jr. (1991). *Beyond race and gender.* New York: AMACOM.

Toffler, A. (1990). *Power shift.* New York: Bantam.

Tregoe, B. B., Zimmerman, J. W., Smith, R. A., & Tobia, P. M. (1989). *Vision in action.* New York: Simon & Schuster.

Viscott, D. S. (1980). *Risking: How to take chances and win.* New York: Simon & Schuster.

Wall, B., Solum, R. S., & Sobol, M. R. (1992). *The visionary leader.* Rocklin, CA: Prima.

Walton, M. (1990). *Deming management at work.* New York: Perigee.

Webster's Dictionary. (1977). (J. G. Allee, Ed.). Baltimore: Ottenheimer.

About the Author

Patricia Arredondo is founder and president of Empowerment Workshops, Inc., of Boston. She developed her organizational consulting practice in 1985 with a special focus on diversity and change management processes. Her work is conducted across industries and serves both for profit and not-for-profit businesses. Her client list includes Ad Club Foundation of Boston, AT&T, Gillette Company, Girl Scouts of the USA, Head Start, Johnson & Johnson Orthopaedics, New York City Public Schools, and Northeastern University. She led the evaluation project of more than 50 diversity initiatives in human services and cultural institutions funded by a consortium of foundations in Boston. A licensed psychologist, she is a former professor at Boston University and the University of New Hampshire. She is a Fellow of the American Psychological Association, president of the Association for Multicultural Counseling and Development (1996-1997) and past president of the Massachusetts Chapter of the National Hispanic Psychological Association. In the Boston area, she serves on numerous boards, including INROADS of Central New England and the Massachusetts School of Professional Psychology. She received her doctorate in counseling psychology from Boston University in 1978.

Printed in the United States
1520900005B/196-210